FATHERLOVE

D. Bruce Lockerbie

FATHERLOVE

Learning to Give the Best You've Got

A DOUBLEDAY-GALILEE ORIGINAL

DOUBLEDAY & COMPANY, INC., GARDEN CITY, NEW YORK
1981

Library of Congress Cataloging in Publication Data

Lockerbie, D. Bruce.
  Fatherlove, learning to give the best you've got.

  "A Doubleday-Galilee original."
  1. Fathers. 2. Parenting. 3. Father and child.
I. Title.
HQ756.L58   649'.1
ISBN: 0-385-15865-3
Library of Congress Catalog Card Number: 80-711

FIRST EDITION

Grateful acknowledgment is made to the following for permission to reprint their copyrighted material.

Excerpt by Robert Coles, copyright © 1979 by *The New Yorker*, magazine. Reprinted by permission.

"The Bee" copyright © 1966 by James Dickey. Reprinted from *Poems 1957–1967* by James Dickey, by permission of Wesleyan University Press.

Excerpt from the poem "Ash-Wednesday" from *Complete Poems and Plays of T. S. Eliot* by T. S. Eliot. Reprinted by permission of Harcourt Brace Jovanovich, Inc., and Faber & Faber, Ltd.

Excerpt from "The Death of the Hired Hand" from *The Poetry of Robert Frost,* edited by Edward Connery Lathem. Copyright 1930, 1939, © 1969 by Holt, Rinehart and Winston. Copyright © 1958 by Robert Frost. Copyright © 1967 by Lesley Frost Ballantine. Reprinted by permission of Holt, Rinehart and Winston, Publishers.

Excerpt from "The Bridge at Dawn" from *New Poems* by Richard Le Gallienne. Reprinted by permission of Dodd, Mead & Company, Inc.

Excerpt by Gail Sheehy, copyright © 1980 by the New York *Times.* Reprinted by permission.

In memory of my father

I have no greater joy than to hear
that my children are walking in the
truth.

3 John 4

Contents

Introduction

What does it mean to be a father? Who can presume to give the answer, inscribed as if by the finger of God? One of the world's great wise men, Sir Francis Bacon, summed up the problems of parenthood in general, fatherhood in particular, with two famous statements. Bacon wrote, "The joys of parents are secret, and so are their griefs and fears: they cannot utter the one, nor they will not utter the other." Bacon also said, "He that hath wife and children hath given hostages to fortune."

Unutterable joy, inexpressible grief. Surely, that's part of what it means to be a father or a mother. But is that all? Are these two extremes of joy and pain a parent's only common experience with other fathers and mothers? Is there no middle ground in which it's possible to speak with moderation about our hopes and aspirations, our fears and doubts, for our children? Must it be true that the unknowable future threatens every father with blackmail?

No one knows all there is to know about being a father—not even Bacon, although he once claimed to have taken all knowledge to be his province; much less do I possess any secret formula for success. All I can do is point to experience and observation and say, "Here are some examples of people who *tried*." After looking at the record of many fathers, however, this much is clear: To be a father means living through life's greatest paradoxes—strength-in-weakness, weakness-in-strength; dependence and independence; individuality of persons and community of family.

Under normal stress, the tensions of living as individuals within a traditional family will challenge our patience and endurance. By definition, participation in family life demands giving of oneself to others. But selfless giving is hardly a characteristic of our society in these closing years of the twentieth century; therefore, as with so many other traditional elements in our civilization, the very idea of "family" has undergone revision. Until recently, our culture took for granted that the term "family" implied a typical social unit made up of husband and wife living together with the children whom their love and marriage had brought into the world. It was also taken for granted that the several roles in this family were clearly defined. Husband-father, wife-mother, and children-students all knew their places and what was expected of them by each other and by society.

Today, of course, so much of this structure has changed, its recounting seems like a case study in primitive anthropology. The most dramatic change is in the number of single-parent families resulting from the current divorce epidemic. Statistics reveal that, unless the present trend reverses, more American couples in the 1980s will be obtaining divorce settlements than marriage licenses. Add to these the increasing number of legal separations or abandonments, plus separation caused by death, and the nature of America's family unit can no longer be stereotyped as consisting of father-mother-son-and-daughter. Consequently, more and more children are growing up in single-parent families with little awareness of the anomaly of their situation; in fact, there are increasingly large segments of our society in which the child whose parents are still living together may be considered a curiosity among his playmates.

Being a father is difficult enough, even with the loving support of a faithful wife and mother. How much more difficult it must be for men without women! But even in those cases in which both parents are in the home, a perplexing sense of being cut off from other people, with their common problems and solutions, sometimes troubles a father. For one man, this sense of distance from his wife and children comes about through her domination over the family; for another, his loneliness is self-imposed, fostered perhaps by a wrong-headed *macho* attitude or cultural misunderstanding of the father's proper role. Similarly, for some women, their own fathers' unfortunate example may altogether color their attitudes toward men; for others, the propaganda and politics of the women's liberation movement may distort their understanding of marriage and the family. The increasing clamor among homosexual men to be allowed to adopt children and by homosexual women to produce their own offspring by means of artificial insemination suggests how far awry modern attitudes toward family structure and fatherhood have taken us.

Some of these modern attitudes are also apparent in popular representations of fathers. Judging from weekly television programming, both re-runs and current series, the unfavorable portrait of fathers remains a constant ingredient in drama and entertainment. The features of a father seen on television are often those of a simpleton or lout, a stumblebum and incompetent, the object of his children's well-deserved disrespect. Soap opera fathers are almost uniformly doctors or lawyers too preoccupied with their professional concerns to know or care about their wives and children; no wonder, then, that these neglected women and teenagers wander into disastrous love affairs and juvenile delinquency. Domestic comedies may offer greater variety in the occupations of fathers, but these men—whether blue-collar workers or Wall Street bankers—are almost universally portrayed as nincompoops. Foremost among them stands Archie Bunker as the prototypical father in American culture: a bigot and racist, a hypocrite and chauvinist, the foil for all his wife's virtues, the dark corner into which the light of his daughter's liberal education must shine.

On the whole, fathers have been subjected to more than enough ridicule—in "Father Knows Best" and "My Three Sons," in "Sanford and Son" and "All in the Family." What today's father needs isn't further abuse from smart-alecks on television or feminists on soap boxes; instead, every father needs encouragement to do and keep on doing what his heart tells him is right—to love his wife and children, to teach his sons and daughters to become persons of character. To help him be this kind of man, every father is looking for a model to emulate, an original pattern to copy in his own life. But, in a world of cheap shots and caricatures demeaning to fathers, where is a man to find what he's searching for?

Certainly not in the spate of books on family relations and "parenting." In a *New Yorker* magazine review of Christopher Lasch's book, *The Culture of Narcissim,* Robert Coles—himself a psychologist—comments on what Lasch calls "the evil of psychologizing." Coles agrees, and his criticism is worth quoting at length:

> Millions of us are caught up in the pretentious jargon of child-rearing guides, manuals, books. All that talk of "parenting." All those psychological explanations, not only naive and sometimes absurd but ephemeral as well—replaced by new guides or contradictory ones: psychology as an instance of consumerism. Is it the first five years that really count, or the first three? And how you handle your child immediately after he or she is born? . . . We want to "analyze" everything, including our children's behavior, and at the same time we have convinced ourselves that we lack the authority to take a firm stand on much of anything—with respect to their lives or our own. A large crew of hustlers has gleefully moved into this moral vacuum, talking "child development" and "human motivation."

Then Robert Coles asks:

> Why do parents rush toward these people, eager for their every pronouncement? What are the implicit promises made, if only one will obey all the rules handed down? We are obsessed with "techniques" in the home, as parents, for the same reason that we turn to the counsel of industrial sociologists, practitioners of "personal management," and "guid-

ance counsellors." All these "experts" are disguised moralists, who want to give us answers and more answers, to put us in our place: Do this, don't do that, lest you be judged "maladjusted," "sick," or "abnormal." The covert nature of their preaching (backed up by considerable political and economic authority) is a measure of how uncomfortable we have learned to be with an open acknowledgment of any moral—never mind spiritual—concerns we may yet have, despite the age and its culture.

This is the secular age; ours is a secular culture, given over to our obsession with temporal and material concerns. In such a culture, the things of the spirit are largely ignored, if not outrightly denied. In addressing our culture, writers like Lasch and Coles may accurately assume that the majority of their readers, as Coles observes, will "regard religion as a joke, as inconsequential, or as a mere ritual." It runs contrary, therefore, to the age and its culture to suggest that the remedy for our national malaise and our individual loss of self-confidence—the remedy for the collapsing of family structure and the melting away of a father's influence—lies in a return to the roots of our religion. But faith in God leads to respect for the institution of the family and recognition of God's special benediction upon fatherhood. We find this demonstrated throughout the pages of the Bible, in its many references to God the Father and his design for family life. Its declarations of responsibilities of parents for children, of fathers for sons and sons for fathers, are spelled out in the Law of Moses, in the Psalms, Proverbs, and Ecclesiastes; in the teachings of Jesus of Nazareth; in the letters of St. Paul. Ultimately, we find the highest standard in the example of God the Father and God the Son, the Lord Jesus Christ. As Christians, we're called to follow this example of the Father's love and the Son's obedience, to become the sort of sons and fathers we were meant to be—made in the image and likeness of the Son and His Father.

No book can hope to speak beyond the experience of its

author—in this case, the husband of one wife, the father of three children, now themselves young adults. Ours is far from being the ideal household; no one who knows us well would ever mistake us for the Holy Family. But in a quarter-century of living together with people whom I love and for whom, under God, I am responsible, I've been able to learn, from my own family and from observation of other families, some of the reasons for my own failures and limited success as a father. This book, then, is an attempt at sharing what I've learned from others—fathers and mothers alike, but also fathers without wives, mothers without husbands, young couples who as yet have no children. For one of the most important lessons I've learned is that, whatever one's situation—whether as married man or as widowed, divorced, or separated parent—no one needs to be cut off from the community of other parents, except by fear. No one needs to blunder through the trauma of being a father, possibly wrecking children's lives, destroying a marriage and, with that destruction, any hope for a tranquil life. From the principles of God's Word, from the example of others who care about us and our children, and from the resources of our own sanctified common sense, help is available to make being a father one of God's great gifts.

D.B.L.

Stony Brook, New York

Acknowledgments

This book would not have been written or published without the help of Alex Liepa, formerly of Doubleday and Company. I am grateful for his encouragement, as well as that of Jan Waring.

Many other persons have also contributed to this book by sharing their experiences and observations with me. To all of them, anonymously, my thanks.

Mary Rost typed and corrected the manuscript. For her work I can never say enough.

But it is primarily to my wife Lory and our children—Don, Kevin, and Ellyn—that I am most indebted, for they are the ones who, by their very being, have made this book possible.

FATHERLOVE

CHAPTER 1

The Blessed Event

"Darling," she says with eyes glowing. "We're going to have a baby!"

Perhaps that joyful news first hits us as a shock. Or maybe the word comes after careful discussion and planning of economic and domestic factors. Are we making enough money to afford a baby now, or should we wait? Is there enough room in this apartment, or will we have to move? Whatever the circumstances, in most cases our feelings are largely the same: a vast, overwhelming sense of pride mixed with sober anticipation.

He reaches out for her, and as she comes eagerly into his arms, he knows the source of his joy at becoming a father. It originates in embracing the woman he loves.

"How do you know?" he whispers.

"Silly! I *know!* Besides, I went to the doctor today, and he says so. That upset stomach I've been feeling the last few days? It isn't the flu, I assure you. It's morning sickness, and it may be around for a few weeks."

"When . . . ?"

"Probably the middle of October. Dr. McIntyre wrote down on my chart, *EDC: October 15.*"

"*EDC?*"

"Expected date of confinement. It's a term doctors use to inform a hospital's maternity ward to expect a customer. Sort of like making a reservation for a hotel at Waikiki Beach."

At the recall of their Hawaiian honeymoon, he holds her

even tighter; then suddenly he releases her. Her eyebrows question.

"I don't want to hurt you or the baby."

She laughs at his caution. "You can't hurt me or the baby by loving us! Just hold me and tell me you're happy."

"Here," she says to her husband one evening, a few months later, "put your hand right here. The baby's kicking."

Her eyes glisten at the realization of her child's life within her, at knowing the steady growth from embryo to fetus to infant.

No man is ever adequately prepared to be a father; at least, not to the same degree he assumes his wife has been prepared to become a mother by the very fact of her womanhood. For a woman, it seems, the marvel of impending motherhood and all that means may not be quite so sudden or alarming as the prospect of fatherhood is for a man. She is, after all, the warm center of life, the specific locus in which new life begins, is nourished through its prenatal existence, and from which, nine months later, a human being emerges. She prepares throughout gestation to welcome her child. As she experiences visible and invisible changes to both her body and her psyche, she comes to know and commune with the reality of another life developing within her womb. She takes an added joy from knowing that her child's complete well-being depends upon her own health and strength. She alone is the source of supply, her body providing the sheltered environment in which the unborn waits for birth.

Her husband cannot begin to comprehend such mystery. He knows little more than this: He loves his wife, and he will love the child she bears because it is theirs. Twenty-five years ago, when I first became a father, there was little thought that a husband might want to share the childbirth experience with his wife —although I once did so without choice! A generation ago, as today, expectant fathers were little more than fit subjects for a TV comedy. Even today, in spite of all the clinical instruction he may receive in advance, for all the well-planned efforts at involving the father in the birthing of his child, the fact remains that most men feel superfluous, decidedly less important than the featured performers in this drama. A man cannot literally enter into his wife's anxieties any more than he can literally know the stretching and tearing of her body as her labor pangs mount to the moment of delivery. He can only assure her of his love, his desire for her comfort, his prayers for her safe passage through the valley of the shadow of death, his love for the baby she will deliver.

At long last—after the months of maternity clothes and baby showers, after poring over lists of names for boys and names for girls, after the classes and the exercise—the moment arrives. Twenty-five years ago, it went something like this.

Three men sit cramped in a tiny room. Its furniture overlaps, leaving almost no space for them to stretch their legs. An aged sofa sags with weariness, its upholstery stained by sweat and hair oil. From under a plastic veneer of imitation leather, the stuffing of a chair leaks out. The only lampshade is askew. A maple table, ring-marked and burned by coffee cups and cigarettes, carries the usual array of last year's magazines. Paint chips peel and fall from the ceiling. No one would choose to sit in this room, but every day men no different from these three come here to wait and wonder and worry.

The men say nothing to each other; an early morning lethargy has replaced their comradery when first they met a few hours before. For no reason, one of the men picks up a copy of a magazine he had only moments ago discarded, leafing through it once again as if looking for something he had lost; then, as before, he tosses it aside and resumes his idleness. A second man, older than the others, his face matted with concern, succumbs to sleep, his head thrown back on the sofa with such awkwardness and strain that the cords of his neck stand out like cables. Exhaustion has overcome any need for comfort. The third man reaches for his cigarettes and finds only an empty pack. With a muttered curse he crumples the Marlboro box into the already overloaded ashtray. Stepping over the legs of the sleeper, over the coffee table, he wanders out into the corridor to find a vending machine.

A snore shudders through the sleeping man, and his restless companion reaches again for a magazine. But as he does, he hears the scuff of footsteps coming from the other end of the corridor. He hesitates a moment, half in, half out of his chair, frozen as if in stop-film. The doorway fills with the form of a man in a white hospital coat, and a voice says, "Congratulations, Mr. Jones! You've got a son!"

There will never be another moment in life quite like that first instant in which a man knows he is a father. Jesus of Nazareth described the ecstasy of every mother in these words: "A woman giving birth to a child has pain because her time has come; but when her baby is born, she forgets the anguish because of her joy that a child is born into the world" (John 16:21). For her husband, the relief may not be physical, but it is no less a lifting of anguish and concern, a rocket ride of exultant joy!

He asks the only two questions that matter. "Is she okay, Doctor? And is everything all right with the baby?"

The obstetrician smiles, nods, and speaks the carefully chosen, professionally appropriate reply, "Everything appears to be just fine. You may go up to the maternity ward in a few minutes to see her."

He doesn't wait for the elevator but dashes up two or three flights of stairs, arriving breathless at a desk where two nurses sit, sipping their morning coffee. "Yes?" inquires one of them, as if addressing an intruding child. "Are you looking for someone?" They have witnessed this scene before, and their only relief from the routine of their work appears to be the ridiculing of each day's new batch of young fathers.

"My wife's just had a baby . . ."

"Name, please."

"Jones." He is still panting from his run up the stairs.

"You *are* Mr. Jones?"

He looks at the nurse with scorn. "No, I'm Captain Kangaroo! Look, I'd just like . . ."

The nurse is neither amused nor hurried by his wit. She con-

tinues to leaf through papers on a clipboard until she comes to
the proper chart.

"Your wife is still in the recovery room. If you'll go back
downstairs to the lobby, we'll call you when we are able to . . ."

"But Dr. McIntyre told me . . ."

"I'm sure Dr. McIntyre told you to wait a few minutes," the
nurse intones in her best schoolma'am's rebuke.

He turns obediently to go. At that moment, the swinging doors
at the end of the corridor part, and a rolling stretcher appears,
flanked by nurses and orderlies wearing their green delivery
room apparel. He knows at once who is on that cart and goes to
her.

"Hi there, Daddy!" she calls to him and reaches for his hand.
"We did it, didn't we?"

"Hi, darling. We sure did!"

The rest of the day passes in a blur. Phone calls to her mother
and brother, both living in a nearby city; to his own parents a
continent away. Flowers to be ordered, a call to the diaper service requesting delivery in three days, a stop at the printer to
order the special birth announcements—no conventional commercial cards for him! By evening visiting hours, his mother-in-
law has arrived to see her first grandchild and spend the next
few days helping her daughter adjust to her new duties. The
son-in-law has mixed feelings about her presence. He appreci-
ates her desire to help her daughter, but something within him
resents the notion that he and his wife and their child still need
parental assistance.

All irritation subsides, however, when he leads his mother-in-
law to the nursery window and motions to the nurse on duty to
wheel his son's bassinet into closer view. Together they agree that
there has never been a more beautiful baby! Then he takes her
arm, and they walk to the semi-private room where the new
mother is sitting up in bed, her face radiant with pride and
fulfillment.

A week or so later, his mother-in-law has returned home, content that her daughter will succeed at performing her new role

as mother. When he hears this kind of talk, however, the young father realizes what has been troubling him throughout her stay. All conversation between mother and daughter seems to have centered around the baby; next comes the home. But what about him? Where does he fit in? And what about her duties as a wife? Not long after they are alone, he allows the subject to invade the blissful spirit of their first evening alone together as parents. Unreasonably and against all his best judgment, he looses upon her his insecurity and frustration. His pettiness swells to a dreadful scene, as insinuation yields to accusation, with neither husband nor wife making sense. For background accompaniment, the baby begins to bawl *fortissimo*. She picks him up, sobbing herself at her husband's foolish misunderstanding. It's more than he can stand to see her cry, and, in total surrender to love, he draws his wife and child to himself. Their tears eventually give way to redeeming laughter, but not before he has caught a glimpse of the new dimensions his life is now assuming. His relationship with his wife hasn't changed, but their loyalty to each other has been enlarged to include another person, an extension of themselves. From this point on, no decision they make can fail to consider its impact on their son and, in time, their other children. For the first time, he begins to understand what it means to be a father.

Does this scenario sound familiar to you? If you've been a participant in the Blessed Event at any time in the last six thousand years, you remember all these details with perfect clarity. You also know where it leads from here. Toilet training and nursery school, tonsillitis and Little League, summer camp and the first fracture, junior high and the first love, senior high and driver ed, College Boards and college admissions; then that weekend when the college sweetheart comes to visit the family, followed by engagement and marriage. It all happens so quickly: One moment, it seems, they're still in diapers; the next, in tuxedo and wedding gown.

On the morning of October 19, 1957, in a Long Island village hospital, my wife Lory gave birth to our firstborn, Donald Bruce

Lockerbie, Jr. We'd moved through various stages of our relationship—from "going steady" in 1952, to courtship, engagement,
and then newly-married bliss a year before. Now we were parents. In striking as well as subtle ways, our life together would
never be quite the same. The love that had brought us together
emotionally and physically had reproduced itself in the form of a
child, a human being for whose existence we were responsible.
Our son. He was an odd looking little gnome, with an alarming
hydrocele, or bulge, on the back of his skull. But we loved him
because he was ours—and in time, the sac of fluid disappeared
altogether. Today he too is a married man, continuing the time-
less cycle of son-and-father-and-son.

In our family, we've brought three children into the world,
two sons and a daughter. Our second son, Kevin John, gave his
mother quite a struggle, almost 24 hours of labor. Eventually we
decided to go to Huntington Hospital that Sunday evening and
wait there for something to happen. But nothing did. At last,
around midnight, Dr. Sewall Pastor told me to go home, and
he'd call when the birth was imminent. I didn't feel like driving
25 miles back to Stony Brook, with the possibility of having to
turn right around and come back. So I called a friend of mine,
Dick Ploth, at that time the assistant minister at Huntington's
Central Presbyterian Church, asking if he had a place where I
could sleep for a few hours. He put me up on a comfortable
couch in his church office, just a few blocks from the hospital;
then he brought in a cot for himself and spent the rest of the
night with me. Next morning, March 16, 1959, at seven-thirty,
when the call came from the hospital, there I was, fully
refreshed and ready to greet the newest member of our family.
Poor Lory hadn't had it so easy! As Kevin himself will tell you—
and his mother will confirm—he had worn her out.

Our daughter's birth was entirely different from her brothers'.
We were living in a duplex apartment in Hegeman Hall, a
boys' dormitory at The Stony Brook School, where my duties—in
addition to teaching English—included conducting the choir.
One Sunday—it happened to be October 9, 1960—I'd been in the

chapel rehearsing the choir for our morning anthem. When I came back to our apartment to escort my wife and sons to the service, Lory told me that she was beginning to have contractions, very slight, nothing worth mentioning.

"Okay, I'll take the boys with me and get someone to look after them; then when the anthem's finished, I'll leave the service and we'll go over to Huntington," I said.

"Oh, no," Lory protested, remembering her prolonged stay in the labor room there the last time. "I don't want to go to the hospital until I'm ready."

So off I went to the service and located the boys' favorite baby-sitter to care for them. I conducted the choir selection and returned to the apartment just in time to hear Lory let out a whoop! Terrified, I called the doctor 25 miles away. While the phone rang, through my mind flashed all the stories I'd ever heard about emergency deliveries. My knees were limp, my heart thundering like a jackhammer. I can remember saying almost out loud, "I've got to boil some water." When Dr. Pastor answered the phone, he advised me, if at all possible, not to expose my wife to a back-seat-of-the-car delivery. "Is there anyone there who can help you?"

Just then, in the door walked our friend Carolyn Dodd, wife of my dormitory colleague Bruce Dodd, whose apartment was just down the hall. Unknown to me, Lory and she had talked earlier while I was at choir rehearsal, and Carolyn, in her thoughtful way, was just checking to see that everything was still all right. So far as I was concerned, everything was very definitely not all right! "Lory's having that baby right now!" I blurted out. Carolyn sprinted up the stairs to the bedroom, calling behind her, "Get Bruce from the chapel! Get the school nurse!"

It would make a much better story if I could say that I delivered our daughter in our apartment bedroom, but it wouldn't be true. While I was running around the campus—dashing to the infirmary to get the nurse, then a block or two away to find the nearest doctor—Carolyn and Bruce Dodd calmly proceeded to turn that bedroom into an obstetrics ward and delivery room. By the time the physician arrived, all he had to do was cut the umbilical cord. Both mother and baby were doing just fine, thank you. When it was time to go to the hospital—better late than never!—the rescue squad from a volunteer fire brigade dropped Lory's stretcher and bounced her down the last few steps of the staircase. But by that time, we were all too overjoyed and relieved to care. We had our little girl, and we named her Ellyn Beth.

The birth of every child in a family has its own significance, but for obvious reasons, the arrival of the firstborn is special; and it can lead to special problems. There's a stranger on the scene. One of the reasons for getting married was so that two lovers could live together, just the two of them, with no concern about other family members to invade their privacy. But all of a sudden, here's an intruder, a very insistent voice demanding constant attention, often at most inconvenient hours of the night.

I remember well those early weeks and months with our baby Don, in the fall and winter of 1957–58: night after night of interrupted sleep, the two o'clock vigil for feeding and burping and changing the baby. He took some getting used to. It wasn't easy to accept the fact that having a child changes the chemical mix of a marriage. We had to learn to make adjustments to our patterns of living. We had to recognize that our freedom as a duo—freedom to come and go as we pleased, freedom to set our own schedules—would now be greatly curtailed since we had become a trio. Did we resent this infringement on our privacy? Did we squawk about losing a few of our treasured privileges as a young couple?

To be perfectly honest, of course we did! In those years I was competing in major track meets, representing the New York Athletic Club almost every weekend, especially during the winter indoor season. The first year of our marriage, Lory had been able to go along and see me run in places like the Boston Garden, Chicago Stadium, Milwaukee Arena, or Philadelphia Convention Hall. I liked knowing that she was there, hearing my name announced at the starting line, cheering me through the laps of the invitational 1,000-yard run or the glamorous one-mile race, sharing my joy or disappointment after the meet. But when the next season came around, our baby was only two-and-one-half-months old, too young to be left repeatedly for an entire weekend, and so I lost my cheerleader at most of the meets. Lory managed to make the Madison Square Garden events in nearby New York City, and once I convinced her to leave Don and come with me again to Boston, where I'd always run well. But this time it wasn't quite the same. She spent much of the weekend wondering how the baby's sniffles were; we quarrelled during the pre-race dinner over whether or not she should call home. I finished last in the Knights of Columbus Mile.

I hope—although one can't be sure—I wasn't silly enough to blame my poor showing on my wife and son; yet, looking back, I certainly can recall other moments of frustration and pique when either Lory or I, or both, may have lost sight temporarily of the wonderful privilege we'd exchanged for self-indulgence: the irreplaceable privilege of parenthood, and the ongoing responsibility that privilege requires.

Responsibility: That's the key word. It comes from an interesting source, the Latin verb meaning "I promise." In Roman times, the *sponsus* was a man engaged to be married, someone who had promised his life and possessions to a specific woman, his *sponsa*. At their wedding the couple exchanged their promises, becoming responsible to and for each other's welfare. This summons to responsibility continues today in traditional marriage vows, in which both bride and groom promise to love, comfort, honor, and keep each other in whatever circumstance of life. But this sense of responsibility, this awareness that one's actions now have consequences for other people, doesn't always arrive automatically at the end of adolescence or with the achieving of voting age. The Reverend Jesse Jackson reminds his audiences of teenaged males, "You're not a man because you can make a baby; you're a man because you can care for a baby, provide for a baby, be a father to a baby."

Responsibility is one of the credentials for adulthood. Automobile insurance companies recognize this fact, especially in the case of young men. They offer better premium rates to men under 25 years of age after they marry; in some instances, even lower rates as they become fathers. Why? Because actuarial statistics show that married men and fathers drive more carefully than their bachelor brothers. Married men and fathers in particular carry with them a greater sense of responsibility, and it grows as their family grows. But for some men, even after marriage, responsibility needs to be nurtured like a delicate flower. For some, perhaps, the full realization of what it means to be responsible—to live by your sworn word of promise—never strikes home clearly until the new father holds his own infant in his arms.

Because of the miracle of love, the birth of a child binds most men closer to their wives than ever before. But not always. Even among those prospective parents who have participated in a prenatal program of instruction and preparation for the husband's new role as father, including his presence in the delivery room, some men feel isolated when the time actually comes. They resent being treated like an outsider by a busy hospital staff. Sometimes that same resentment continues long after the father has left the hospital cashier's window and taken wife and baby home. In some cases, that feeling of isolation parallels a fear that the arrival of a child may become a wedge that drives husband and wife apart.

"That's why I never wanted to have kids," says Paul, a young husband and father now awaiting divorce from his wife Joyce and their five-year-old son Brad. "Children make me uncomfortable. I'm not at ease around them. Oh, I know what people say: You learn to love your own kids and, through them, other people's also. But it's not that way with me."

"I'll take the blame, if that's what it is," says Joyce. "Yes, I insisted on having a child, even though I knew how Paul felt about it. He'd say, 'I like our life the way it is. We don't need anybody else to love. We have each other.' But I never really took him seriously. I kept thinking how he'd change his mind the first time he held his own child in his arms."

Joyce tightens her shoulders and bites her lower lip in anguish. "I had no idea how threatened he'd be, how jealous of my holding our son next to me. I really think Paul hates Brad for robbing him of some of my love."

"Joyce reads too many books on psychology," says Paul hotly, "and I won't accept that Oedipus-complex garbage. I'm not jealous of my son; I just don't think he needs all her time. When I wanted the two of us to go out for an evening, the way we used to, I'd always get the same song and dance about leaving the baby too often with a sitter. Joyce became like somebody straight out of a TV comedy, *smothering* her kid instead of mothering him. And where did that leave me? I felt more and more like an outsider in my own home, so I just took off."

"Yes, maybe I read too much psychology," Joyce retorts, "but Paul could use a lesson in logic. There's such a thing as cause and effect. He brought it on by his change of attitude toward me. He never showed the same affection for me after Brad and I came home from the hospital. It was almost as though he'd caught me being unfaithful to him. He became so cold, he'd never touch me when I was holding the baby. He acted as though breast-feeding was dirty and should be done in the bathroom. So, I admit it," Joyce says through her tears, "I turned more and more of my loving and caring toward my son because he responded to that love."

Did parenthood wreck Paul's and Joyce's marriage? Perhaps, although it's also possible that any marriage in which love and understanding can be jettisoned so easily was already headed for the rocks. How could an event that brings most couples glad tidings of great joy mean disaster for Paul and Joyce? Why was Paul so reluctant to become a father?

For some men, the responsibilities of fatherhood are simply more than they bargained for. It's not just the intrusion of a newborn child's demands; not just the fearful anticipation of financial burdens, from crib to college. Rather, it's the stark reality that the honeymoon has come to an end. Accompanying that reality may be the fear that, with the onset of family life and the responsibilities of parenthood, the feast of love will grow stale, the wine of love will lose its bouquet. Often, when a man is insecure about himself, afraid of his personal attributes as a husband and lover, he's unable to perceive a marvelous truth about marriage: The love between husband and wife possesses a miraculous ingredient that makes possible the expansion of that love to include others.

However, we all know that today many couples disagree with this position and, of course, it's not for you or me to judge another man and woman's choice. All I can say is that the Bible makes it clear that God our Creator, having made us in his image and likeness, intends for us to "be fruitful and increase in number." In giving life and love to a child, whether by birth or by adoption, we participate most nearly in what it means to be made in God's image because then we share—if only to a limited degree—the chiefest attributes of God the Father himself. Not to offer love to our own children is to miss one of the foretastes of eternity, the grace of posterity as a sacrament of everlasting life. For to change Macbeth's awful vision of his damnation into a glorious prospect, what could be more fitting than a line of heirs to God's goodness in Creation, stretching out till the call to our Eternal Home?

But even when a man wants children, some men discover that they aren't ready for and can't meet the responsibilities of being a father. They find they just can't cope with the adult world. Stan is such a man. Not long ago he seemed happily married to his college sweetheart—a Suzy Cheerleader, a charming little pixie, coy, kittenish, and seeming to be utterly dependent on Stan. Throughout their courtship and early period of marriage, Stan had treated Eileen like the co-ed idol worshiper she'd always been. Stan had been the stereotypical Big Man on Campus, the All-Conference defensive end whom nobody pushed around. He made all the decisions. "Eileen is the cutest little airhead I know," he'd say, while his wife merely giggled and tossed her Dorothy Hamill hair-do.

But after maternity, Eileen took on an entirely different personality. Stan could see that she was no longer the little girl who needed her masculine behemoth to lead her by the hand through life. Instead, she was a thoroughly competent woman—a person who had given life to another human being. She now thought of herself with more respect and insisted on it from her husband. She cringed at the idea of being dehumanized into Stan's toy. She was capable of making decisions that affected not only herself but also the welfare of her husband and child. She demanded to be let out of the Doll's House.

All this was too much for Stan. Eileen's strength of character astonished him—terrified him, in fact. He didn't know how to respond to a woman who had a mind of her own and was determined, even belatedly, to exercise it. He retreated away from his masculine image of superior strength, away from the decisive husband and protector. He was not equipped to share the role of parent with his wife; so he regressed to a level more fitting to his emotional level of maturity: He left Eileen and went back to live with his mother.

For reasons of their own, Eileen and Stan will not consider a divorce or even the formality of a legal separation. He comes every Saturday to the house he still owns and maintains to cut the lawn or do other necessary chores. Sometimes Stan stays for Saturday night supper with Eileen and their daughter Barbara. Then he returns home to his widowed mother because, as Stan puts it, "She really needs me." Clearly, Stan prefers being a son to being a father.

But more often than not, the reason why some men fear to become fathers is their deep sense of inadequacy and their fear of failure. Talk about helplessness! The infant in the cradle, certainly; but have you recently watched a young father in his first attempts at changing diapers? All of us are so new at the business of being parents, so dependent upon each other, so afraid of failing in the eyes of others, so uptight about not repeating our own parents' errors—perhaps so unsettled by conflicting advice we've read in books or heard from television's experts on child psychology. It's natural, of course, to want to be an exemplary father, a model mother, a pair of parents whose children will grow up loving and respecting us: the All-American Mom and Dad!

The trouble is, there are no such people! Not since Adam and Eve blew it with their firstborn Cain—and before him, in their personal disobedience to God—has there been a father or mother who has done the perfect job of rearing children. Let's admit, in complete honesty, that none of us can ever say, "I've never made a mistake in bringing up my kids." Every one of us has those moments of reflection when we recall an incident we'd far rather forget and say, "If I had a chance to do it over again, I'd do it better next time." Once we've faced up to our own fallibility, the trick is to avoid repeating those blunders.

The basic problem with being parents, of course, is that until it happens we've got no firsthand experience to fall back on. True, we've all had parents, but *having* isn't the same as *being*. And just that fact alone is enough to make some of us panic. Being a father and mother is one drama on the stage of life for which there's no dress rehearsal; you're always right out front in full spotlight, and if you muff your lines the whole world seems to know. Being parents calls upon us to ad lib our way through life, improvising on a familiar theme with variations and embellishments for every reprise, responding to every impromptu demand for an encore. Or, to put it another way, being parents is a lot like walking a high wire: the only way to keep your balance is to look ahead.

Admittedly, being a parent is serious business. But, as every tightrope walker knows, you can't take your aerial act too grimly. For Philippe Petit to make it across the void between the twin towers of the World Trade Center in downtown Manhattan, he had to allow his body to remain flexible, not resisting the wind like a tree—for in some gales, even the strongest trees can be blown over—but dipping and bending at the knees, accommo-

dating to the pressures, while at the same time remaining stead-
fast in purpose. It's the same for parents. Rigid, unyielding fathers and letter-of-the-law mothers may convince themselves
that style produces content, that discipline without even reasonable compromise results in character, that toughness alone creates
good behavior. My experience tells me otherwise. Some of the
sorriest upbringing I know has been by fathers who treat their
children like a drill instructor with a squad of Marine recruits; or
mothers who behave like harridans, screaming at their toddlers
in a supermarket, "I'm going to kill you!" As parents, we need to
be earnest and caring and committed to our task without losing
sight of the humor of our situation. For make very certain of
this: Either we laugh with our children or, in time, they will
laugh at us and our follies.

We also need to avoid trying to do a task for which we have
no preparation or experience, just because we feel that it's our
parental duty. We may be getting in over our heads. I recall a
literal instance of my metaphor. When Don was only eight
months old, Lory and I took him one day to a beach alongside
Stony Brook's harbor. A channel has been dredged for the boat-
ing traffic, but at that time no floating markers warned the
waders. At high tide the bottom dropped suddenly from shin
depth to twelve or fifteen feet of rapidly coursing water. My parents were with us that day, and so Dad and I took Don down to
the water to splash and play. I was holding the baby facing his
mother and grandmother on the beach, my back to the channel
and its swift current. As my son kicked and splashed in glee, I
moved my feet to keep my balance—and was engulfed! I fought
back upward, holding Don at full arms' length. My father—no
swimmer—struggled to reach us. Lory and my mother screamed
and ran toward the water, while Dad and I flailed to keep the
baby from drowning. In God's providence, someone from a passing boat saw our desperation and dived in to help save the baby.
Then it was Dad who was in trouble. The memory of that incident terrifies me all over again.

But isn't that just the way we fathers all too often conduct ourselves? We over-react to the abundance of obligations and re-

sponsibilities of parenthood, assuming that we must handle all teaching and training, all nurture and discipline. If we don't, we somehow fear, we'll lose face with our children. Yet the time comes when we must delegate much of this responsibility to teachers and others involved in our children's formal schooling. We do this, usually, for two reasons: first, because the law requires school attendance; second, because we wisely recognize our own inability to teach our children all they need to know. Our training and experience are too limited, our credentials inadequate. Since we willingly accept the fact of compulsory schooling, with both its assets and liabilities, why balk at accepting the assistance of other adults from whom our children can learn informally, away from the classroom? Why must we feel burdened to do the whole job ourselves?

One Sunday evening, a dozen and more years ago, Lory and I attended a program at our church. This program presented the work with boys in our community done by an organization called Christian Service Brigade. Both our sons were regulars in the Tuesday night Brigade meetings and would be taking part in the presentation that evening. The local leader, a Grumman Engineering Corporation executive named Al Mead, explained to the audience of parents the various aspects of their weekly meetings—recreation, sports, instruction in camping and other outdoor skills, singing, Scripture memorization, and lessons in Christian principles.

Then, addressing us fathers especially, Al Mead made a striking point. He introduced his staff of volunteers, who led each week's activity, by saying, "We're not trying to take over any of the responsibilities you have to your own sons. We just want to see them grow up to be men with strong Christian faith and character. If you don't provide that example, somebody else must!" With a smile in my direction, he clinched his point by adding, "Some of us can teach English, but we don't know one end of the hammer from the other. We want your sons to learn that too!"

I've never forgotten those remarks; in fact, they probably triggered in me the desire to write this book. Certainly it comes close to what I was trying to express in another book, *Who Edu-cates Your Child?* There, as I began to think about my own ex-perience as both boy and man, the metaphor of life's highway stood out in my mind. Those counselors and friends who have helped me on my way by giving guidance and direction seem to me like "living milestones." So I wrote,

> In short, the journey of my life has been marked along the way by encounters with teachers—some academic, others athletic or spiritual mentors—whom God has used to be the guideposts of my life. . . . In my experience, teachers have been more than models to emulate; some have also been like living mile-stones, showing the way ahead, recalling me from detours and aimless wanderings to follow the better course.

All of us have known men and women who have come into our lives as "living milestones." Of course, we parents remain primarily responsible for our children's nurture, but since we've become parents, Lory and I have realized more and more how important it is to have known the blessing of help from others in bringing up our children

- a colleague who shows a child how to build a camp fire and cook a meal
- a neighbor whose gardening teaches respect for the earth
- a coach who teaches the importance of setting high goals
- a skilled carpenter who shows the value of taking pride in one's work
- a friend in whom a teenager can confide
- a teacher whose personal interest carries beyond the classroom, even beyond graduation, in writing letters of en-couragement
- a pastor whose willingness to answer difficult questions helps to validate and stabilize faith.

None of us can do the entire job of being a father alone; we need each other's help, and there's no disgrace in that admission. The only shame comes from not acknowledging our need.

CHAPTER 2

My Father, My Father

Mark Twain reportedly said, "When I was fourteen years old, I thought my father was a fool. But by the time I was twenty-one, I was amazed at how much the old man had learned in the last seven years!" Many sons have had the same experience. Looking backward, we can see, at first, only the faults and follies of others; then often comes a newfound appreciation for our fathers. Curiously, this revised opinion frequently coincides with facing up to the responsibilities of fatherhood for oneself.

In my own case, my attitude toward my father at age twenty-one differed from my attitude at fourteen precisely because in seven years my circumstances had changed so strikingly. With those changes had come responsibilities I now held in common with my father. At fourteen, I was still in high school, immature and irresponsible. But by twenty-one, I was a beginning teacher and coach, responsible for the instruction of my students and athletes. More important, I was also a husband and expectant father, responsible for the welfare of my wife and our unborn child. Suddenly, I realized that there was a lot my father could teach me, in spite of any mistakes he might have made along the way.

My earliest recollections of my father are of him at work on his sermon for Sunday, sitting at his desk in the parsonage room designated as his study, surrounded by books, with a large Bible open on his knee. At those times he wasn't to be disturbed, although I was permitted to play on the floor at his feet, reconstructing the Tower of Babel with piles of books taken from his shelves. Next, I see him in his pulpit, a dynamic, captivating speaker to any audience, young or old; by turns humorous, provocative, challenging, compelling. As I grew older, I came to know other preachers' sons who cringed in embarrassment whenever their fathers took to the pulpit. I never knew that distress, for I never recall being either bored or chagrined by my father's preaching. I consider him still to be among the best I ever heard.

He was always proud to be a Lockerbie, a Scots-Canadian whose ancestors had shared the same valley with King Robert the Bruce. He was quick to correct anyone's misspelling the name by ending it "-by," pointing out the legend that the Lockerby branch of the family had defected before the Battle of Bannockburn, in 1314, to fight with the hated English. From the occasional burr in my father's speech, one might have assumed that he himself was a recent expatriate from Dumfriesshire. But the fact is that he never saw the sheepherding town of Lockerbie, on highway A74 in the south of Scotland, or Robert the Bruce's birthplace at nearby Lochmaben, until he was past fifty years old.

His own father—my grandfather whom I never knew—had been a second-generation Canadian, born in the farming country north of the St. Lawrence River in Eastern Ontario. When asthma forced him to abandon farming, Pearson Lockerbie crossed the St. Lawrence to New York State, where his first son, John Herbert Lockerbie, was born. But Pearson Lockerbie was never meant for the mills and foundries of Buffalo, and so he and his wife Cora returned to the Ontario river-village of Iroquois. There, on Christmas Eve of 1913, my father was born in a house since swept away by the St. Lawrence Seaway Project.

He hated his given names, Ernest Arthur, allowing "Ernie" only to a few friends, his family, and my mother; to all others he was simply E. A. Lockerbie. This name he doodled in his ninth-grade textbooks, along with the names of current sweethearts. Soon thereafter, his boyhood ended, and with it his identity as Ernest Arthur Lockerbie, when he dropped out of Central Collegiate Institute in Hamilton, Ontario, leaving his now-widowed mother's home at 171 East Avenue South. He would make his own way in the world, which for him began in that seeming metropolis called Toronto, some forty miles away. He lived in rooming houses, and while I never learned any of the vivid details of those years, he gave me to understand that his behavior was reckless and irresponsible, particularly in his relationships with women. Like the young man in the parable of the Prodigal Son, he too had wandered into a far country and was wasting his life in riotous living.

His stock-in-trade would always be his personal charm, and with this undeniable asset, he presented himself as a man when he was really still just a boy of sixteen. He made his living as a salesman. In those early years of the Great Depression, when many men were out of work and living on the dole called "city relief," my father's sales pitch could bring him commissions amounting to seventy-five dollars a week. He never gave up selling, in one form or another. The language of salesmanship penetrated into his preaching, as when he would invite his listeners to "close in with God's offer of mercy."

Ironically, it was his romantic charm that turned his life in a new direction. A customer on his door-to-door rounds had a daughter to whom my father was attracted. By charming her mother, he hoped for an opening to ask the daughter for a date. In time his patience was rewarded by an invitation to Sunday dinner. He arrived at the appointed hour, late in the afternoon, enjoyed the meal, and was hoping for some time alone with the young woman, when her mother announced that it was time to go to the evening church service.

My father wasn't unfamiliar with the habit of going to church on Sunday, although since leaving home he'd abandoned the practice himself. His upbringing had been nominally Presbyterian; indeed, as a consequence of the family minister's trip to the Holy Land, my father had been baptized as an infant with water from the Jordan River, a fact his mother seemed to feel merited a certain measure of boasting. Sunday in his boyhood home had been "the Sabbath," a day when the piano bench hid all the popular sheet music, with only the Psalter on display. For Presbyterians in Canada, Sunday was a weekly reiteration of gloom and doom, an attitude, by the way, which my father was never entirely able to shake off, long after he had ceased to sing the psalms.

The church that evening turned out to be the famous Earls' Court Citadel of The Salvation Army, with its world-renowned band. Ernie Lockerbie, who always had a good ear for music, had never before experienced anything like it in connection with religion. Here was a taste of joy altogether missing from the somber expressions of worship he'd been taught as a child. The boom of the bass drum, the flare of cornets, the mellow warmth of trombones reached deep within him so that he found himself forgetting even the young woman next to him, so engrossed was he in listening to the music and then to the spoken message. It was a sermon based on the story in John 9 of the blind man healed by Jesus of Nazareth. Like that man who now could say, "Lord, I believe," my father was being summoned for the first time in his life to believe in Jesus Christ, and he was ready to respond.

Just as the sermon ended, however, and an appeal for commitment began, a burly Salvation Army officer stepped across the aisle to the pew Ernie Lockerbie occupied. Grabbing the young visitor by his lapels, the old Salvationist breathed a firestorm of halitosis into my father's face and shouted, "Young man, you're lost and going to hell!" In shame and disgust, my father shook himself loose from the blunderer and stormed out of the hall into the night. He didn't wait for his companion but walked to his lodgings, enraged at everyone, including himself. But as he walked, a strange thing was happening: His rebellious spirit was being shattered by realizations of how wasted his life had become. By the time he reached his room, he was ready to yield his life in faith to Jesus Christ.

Soon after, he returned to Hamilton, where he met a group of young people who had also recently come to believe in Jesus Christ as Saviour. Among them were several men who felt that

God might be calling them into service as pastors and missionaries—George Darby, Frank Humphreys, Joe Muchan, and John Honeyman, who with his sister Jeanette had recently arrived in Canada from Fifeshire, Scotland. Together these young people rejoiced in their newly declared faith—singing, witnessing, holding open air meetings on Hamilton's streets, preaching in rescue missions. Their friendships developed out of their common joy. In October 1934, Jeanette Honeyman and Ernie Lockerbie were married. A few months later, having committed themselves to serve God wherever and however possible, they found themselves almost at the end of civilization, in Capreol, a tiny railroad junction town in Northern Ontario. There the Canadian National's trains from east and west met. A few yards beyond Capreol's tracks and roundhouses lay the virgin forest, from which black bears came to assert their rights to the berry bushes in the villagers' back yards. Winters were so harsh and snow so deep that dog sleds were the only means of local travel, although the daily train plowed through in all weather.

To this isolated place on the twentieth-century frontier, my father and mother went as home missionaries, combatting both religious indifference and religious antagonism. The latter came especially from French-Canadian Roman Catholic priests who held their people in thrall. There, in August 1935, I was born; from Capreol, a year later, my father was carried, broken in health by his efforts at building an evangelical church in that hostile setting. He returned to Hamilton to recover his strength, although he would carry the effects of angina pectoris for the rest of his life.

For a short time he resumed his career as a salesman, but he knew his calling was to preach, and by the time my sister Jeannie was born, in 1938, he had become the pastor of the Lake Gospel Church in Hamilton, directly across the street from the Dominion Steel foundries. At that time, only two men in his congregation had steady employment; the rest were on relief. Dad's salary amounted to six or seven dollars each week, and with rent to pay and other expenses, not much remained for the food budget. But because of hardship, God proved himself in ways never understood when money is plentiful and need is of little consideration. Young as I was, I learned—at first, unconsciously, then as an article of faith—to believe that, with St. Paul, I could rely on the promise that God meets all my needs, "according to his glorious riches in Christ Jesus" (Philippians 4:19).

Dad was always restless with that kinetic energy of someone never satisfied, someone constantly in pursuit of aspiration's elusive fulfillment. Even after his selling line changed from Wonder Bread to the Bread of Life, he seemed possessed by urges to move on, always to move on. As a result, before "mobility" became part of sociological jargon, our family had moved frequently—from village to town, from town to city, from province to state, from country to country—eight times in my first fifteen years. Sometimes there were additional moves-within-moves, as when the congregation sold one parsonage and bought another. My mother became well acquainted with the ways of Allied Van Lines or their competitors; my sister Jeannie and I accustomed ourselves to starting over again in new schools midway through a term. For me, there were almost a dozen schools before I obtained a high school diploma.

My father never seemed concerned about our apparent rootlessness as a family. To him it was certainly no liability. What other children knew so much geography or had seen so many historical sites at first hand? He was right. Of course we enjoyed great advantages other children of the World War II era never experienced. Whereas other men were in combat in Europe or the Pacific, our father was at home—reluctantly, to be sure, having several times attempted to enlist as a chaplain and being turned down by doctors who knew his medical history. As a preacher, however, he was entitled to gasoline and tires beyond normal wartime rationing quotas, so that while other families were temporarily grounded for the duration, we traveled seemingly at will. I remember a trip, for instance, from Michigan to New York City in the summer of 1945, before V-J Day. No one else in my school had seen the Empire State Building or the Statue of Liberty!

In subsequent summers, we drove once to North Carolina, again to Louisiana and Florida, and one summer spent eight weeks at eight different Bible conferences, from Indiana to the Atlantic provinces of Canada. For my father such summers meant revelling in the thrill of preaching in the Billy Sunday Tabernacle at Winona Lake or being the guest speaker for a week at a conference in the Finger Lakes district of New York State. But in between might lie 500 miles of pell-mell driving long before the era of interstate highways. On these jaunts both eating and sleeping would be catch-as-catch-can. Our custom was to buy a jar of peanut butter and a loaf of bread to make sandwiches, for Dad despised roadside cooking if it involved so much as lighting a can of Sterno. As for restaurants, who could afford them? Dad's honorarium barely paid the travel costs to the next stop. Besides, my mother disapproved of the most common eating-places available, roadhouses advertizing with neon champagne glasses. "It has lights," she'd say, and my father would speed on, while my sister and I in the back seat groaned in hunger. The same was true of most tourist cabins with their sleazy signboards—there were no motels like Holiday Inn as we know them today—and so it wasn't unusual for us to sleep in the car.

As I say, this was my father's style, to be relentlessly active. He disparaged the preference of men like his brother-in-law John Honeyman, who chose to purchase a summer cottage on Lake Huron's Ontario shore and spend his summer vacations there year after year. We often visited our relatives at Kincardine, but our stay was seldom longer than overnight because we were en route to someplace else. Twice, as I recall, Dad tried to accommodate himself to our desires to enjoy our cousins' kind of summer: He rented a lakeside cottage nearby. Both times he barely survived the boredom of settling down for a week at most.

He carried this same passionate need to keep on the move into his pastorates. Wherever he served as pastor of fundamentalist, often independent, Baptist churches in Ontario and Michigan, in New York, Washington, or California, he seemed always attracted most by the call of a congregation in ruins—its unity smashed by some silly quarrel, its mortgage overdue, its youth programs dwindling, its future evidently hopeless. This was the place for E. A. Lockerbie's enthusiasm and vigor; here he would pour out his whole strength in the task of reknitting broken fragments and resuscitating that church's dying spirit.

His method never failed. As soon as the moving van had delivered our goods to the parsonage, Dad set about to introduce himself to the community-at-large. He ignored the fact that his new flock may have been a cause for jibe or even scandal; all that was history. The new preacher joined the volunteer fire department, cheered loudly at the local high school games, presented himself before civic groups, let the neighborhood police precinct know that he was available for ministerial services in any emergency. He also visited constantly—every new family in the vicinity, the elderly in nursing homes, the sick in nearby hospitals; he stopped at every bedside, not only those of his own congregation. He brought together in reconciliation people who hadn't spoken to each other for years. In short, he restored the sense of *koinonia*, the bond of partnership, that had been missing for so long. As a result, people felt good again about going to church.

The real attraction that drew them to attend his church was the magnetism of E. A. Lockerbie's preaching. He may not have looked the part of a clergyman; his dress was often flamboyant. On the road—in a tent revival crusade or in some vast auditorium for a city-wide evangelistic campaign—he might affect a garish plaid suit with a brilliantly colored necktie jutting out from under his prominent chin. The same attire might be seen on Sunday evening in his own church. At such times he looked the part of a traveling salesman. But even on Sunday mornings, his apparel, while more formal, was no more reserved. He would dress in swallowtail coat and striped trousers with a matching cravat

and cement-starched wing collar. Only a boutonniere was missing, because Dad was allergic to flowers of any kind.

Whatever his costume, the effect of his preaching was the same: People were moved to respond. His manner seemed so self-assured and appealing, his power over an audience secure in its total attention to the words that came spilling out like a torrent. Every gesture, every intonation tightened the grip in which he held his listeners, so that even breathing seemed to have stopped. His stamina was astonishing as he strode the platform, for he was never confined to lecturing from behind a lectern. He was a preacher! His art was the rhetoric of persuasion; his calling, to be a watchman on the walls, a herald bringing the Good News. He knew how to wring the human heart and quicken the deadened conscience. As he reached his sermon's moment of climax, perhaps with a convincing story or a dramatic fragment of poetry, few who heard E. A. Lockerbie preach could forever resist his message of hope and deliverance. Even now, I can hear him whispering a favorite clinching stanza, and a chill of loving memory goes through me:

When at last the peace of pardon did her sinking soul restore,
And love sprang up spontaneous that she could not force before;
When she took the place of sinner and at Mercy's footstool lay,
Then he took the place of Saviour, and her burdens rolled away.

But if he was acclaimed for his preaching, my father was somewhat less successful as a pastor. He was an autocrat, perfectly convinced of the rightness of his own views, unwilling to yield an inch of ground in compromising his opinions. As shepherd, he sometimes pushed and shoved his sheep in the direction he wanted the flock to move. Temperamentally he was well suited to the polity of his fundamentalist Baptist churches, with their treasured independence from bishops or other ecclesiastical overseers. In his own congregation, my father was a law unto himself, and he preferred to rule rather than merely reign.

Dad expected people to know their place, as he knew his, and meet their obligations without questioning the authority under which they served. This was true whether they were deacons, trustees, Sunday School teachers, musicians, choir members, or persons in the pew. He would brook no interference from underlings; he was strictly a no-nonsense type who tolerated very little in the way of discussion or rebuttal. This aggressive style rode roughshod over other people's ideas, creating against him understandable resentment which then sometimes overflowed upon his family.

When I was in sixth grade, we were living in a tiny Michigan village called Haslett, now a suburb of East Lansing. Dad was pastor of the only church in town, but really he was more like the mayor: serving on the volunteer fire department, playing center field on the town's baseball team, conducting Monday morning assemblies in the high school, and counseling students in the principal's office. On the surface everything seemed to be going smoothly. Unknown to me, however, deep animosities prevailed within the church leadership, and some of this bad feeling was directed against the pastor. One day, in the locker room at school, an older boy with whom I'd always been friendly shouted at me so that everyone could hear, "My father hates your father, and he's gonna run him out of our church!" Stunned, I stumbled from the locker room in tears, trailing behind me the other boys' derision. It was my first awakening to the fact that my father was not universally loved and respected as the infallible person I took him to be.

At home, there was never any questioning of his authority. My father's characteristic domination of everyone around him carried over into his dealings with his family. When he spoke the word of command, my sister and I responded with alacrity, if not always with cheerfulness. In compliance with St. Paul's words to Timothy, my father hewed to much the same line with us as with his congregation. Children, like church members, were to be seen and not heard, particularly if what the child presumed to say might contradict his elders. My father took his

Bible literally, especially Proverbs 13:24, "He who spares the rod hates his son," so that there was never any doubt in my mind about my father's devoted affection for me! I knew that his anger had a quick fuse, and I learned early to avoid if at all possible the spark that would ignite it. If, for instance, in his judgment it was time for bed, no matter what game I was playing or what radio program I was enjoying I went submissively without teasing or tantrum. I knew better.

Furthermore, our upbringing was expected to be a model of instruction for other parents in the congregation to measure their success or failure in child-rearing. Not infrequently, as I recall, I was singled out for public punishment. No doubt I deserved whatever I got, but I might have preferred not being used as an instrument of rebuke to other parents whose children were perpetrating the same crimes. Perhaps my most memorable experience as scapegoat occurred one Sunday morning when I was about seven years old. For some reason I must have had an inadequate breakfast before going off to Sunday School and the morning worship service that followed. By the time the celebration of the Lord's Supper had concluded, my stomach was crying out for food; yet I could tell by the long line of congregants at the church door that it would be some time before this preacher's kid got his Sunday dinner. And so, accompanied by another boy my age, I edged my way down the aisle of the sanctuary to the communion table where a quantity of bread and grape juice—would Jesus have condoned anything else?—remained in its consecrated state. To me that morning, these humble elements had no particular transcendence, no mystery of Real Presence. They were simply food and drink, and I was famished! I stuffed my mouth with bits of bread and was about to wash them down, when retribution struck. I'd been too busy to notice my father's swift arrival. No need to bore you with further details of that encounter, except to say that later on I was informed that most of the punishment I'd received was for the benefit of the deacon and his wife, whose son had been my confederate in wrongdoing and who had looked on while sacrilege continued.

Was he the perfect father? Of course not. He probably took himself much too seriously in the role; however, who am I to judge? As I say, I'm more sympathetic to my father's faults since discovering a few of my own in that same department. My wife, my mother, or my sister hardly need to remind me that, more and more often, I sound just like my father—querulous, impatient, demanding, contemptuous of the incompetence of bureaucratic functionaries; in short, not the type to suffer fools gladly. My grown sons and daughter, recalling their childhood, can joke now about my foibles; yet even as they do, certain instances in my memory give me little cause for pride. For me, as for my father, most mistakes I've made in child-rearing have begun by adhering to the letter rather than the spirit of the law. But this much must be said for my father: He never neglected to give me the sort of upbringing the Bible recommends, an upbringing that understands why sparing the rod is the same as hating the child.

CHAPTER 3

The Toughest Job Is Building Character

It's always interesting to note how generous we become toward others and their failings after we've had a taste of disappointment with ourselves. That's called "learning the hard way," and unfortunately, it seems to be the way most of us learn best about being a father. We're no longer casual observers, viewing the problems of parenthood, the phenomena of fatherhood, with a sociologist's dispassionate interest. We're involved ourselves—changing diapers, mixing formula, burping the baby, taking photographs, making decisions, working overtime to support our growing family—so proud, someone would think we'd been personally in charge of creating such a miracle! But it isn't all thrills and glowing excitement, for in the quiet moments of anxiety and concern, we realize sooner or later that being a parent—especially being a father—is the toughest job in the world.

In his letters, St. Paul leaves no doubt in his readers' minds as to what a Christian father's responsibilities are to his children: "Bring them up in the training and instruction of the Lord" (Ephesians 6:4). Paul uses two strong words in addressing these Ephesian fathers, *paideia* and *nouthesia,* "training" and "instruction." *Paideia* comes from the Greek verb meaning "to educate." But *paideia* is more than formal schooling, which a child might receive from a *didaskalos* or teacher and whose method probably consisted of rote memorization. Instead, *paideia* suggests a much broader range of methods leading to the desired result, namely a child's good upbringing. Among these methods must be included nurture, correction, and chastening, all of which may be summed up in the single word *discipline*.

Similarly, Paul's word *nouthesia* connotes far more than the casual exchange of ideas and opinions or the transmitting of information that marks so much of our modern schooling; on the contrary, Paul refers to an education based upon *principles,* an education that carries with it admonition and warning. In fact, this word *nouthesia* derives from a combination of two Greek words suggesting both an attentive and a retentive mind. So then, "training" means *discipline,* and "instruction" means the building of principles into a person's character by means of concentrated and repeated lessons. One of the ways in which a child knows that his father loves him is this: When the father speaks, the child listens—or else! The child develops an understanding of his father's methods of "training and instruction." He knows that the father doesn't waste his child's time, doesn't deceive him with double-talk, doesn't intentionally mislead him with false teaching. The father cares for his child; so he makes sure that the child learns carefully and correctly those lessons that the father knows to be essential. When the child falters or makes a mistake, the father lovingly rebukes and requires the child to begin again.

Paideia and *nouthesia.* Maybe it's all Greek to some people, but to any father who really cares about his children, nothing is of greater importance than their training for discipline, their instruction in principles. Together these make up their *character,* which Aristotle defined as the decisions a person makes when the choice is not obvious. My father used to say, "Character is the way we act when nobody's looking." For example, it's no test of character to stop your car at a police roadblock. The test comes, rather, when you're driving at four o'clock in the morning along a desolate back road in Iowa. You're heading toward a red light at a deserted intersection, and you can see for miles around that there's nobody else on the roads. Do you obey the law, even though there's no cross traffic, or zoom on through at full speed? This is a test of character, a choice made on the basis of respect for law, on the discipline of adhering to the principles of safe driving. You decide to stop on the strength of character instead of responding to convenience or whim. Of course, to the person who is well disciplined in respect for law, as well as other ethical and moral principles, such a simple illustration of choice is automatically invalid. For such a person, the only course of action is already established because *you stop at red lights;* that's all there is to it, whatever the time or traffic conditions. Only for a medical emergency does a driver consider some other option, in response to some higher law. In either case, you do what is right, not what you know to be wrong.

But where does such ingrained knowledge of right and wrong come from? Where does a child learn to make such choices? From a father's training and instruction. This job belongs to every parent, but in a special way God has chosen the father of each family to be his representative in the home. We see this in the way that Moses gave the Law of God in Deuteronomy 4–6. Just as their fathers before them had instructed their sons, so these men of Israel were being summoned to teach a new generation of sons the ways of truth.

Hear, O Israel: The Lord our God, the Lord is one. Love the Lord your God with all your heart and with all your soul and with all your strength. These commandments that I give you today are to be upon your hearts. Impress them on your children. Talk about them when you sit at home and when you walk along the road, when you lie down and when you get up (Deuteronomy 6:4–7).

For the ancient Israelites, mere piety wasn't enough; personal devotion and a formal adherence to the Law of God weren't enough. One had to be responsible for others as well. Each father was expected to live up to his divinely appointed obligation, spelled out by God to Moses. The father had to imbue his children with the spirit of the Law so that it became a part of their walk and talk, wholly integrated into every aspect of their conscious and unconscious behavior. To be a Jew meant living in

this knowledge, that a hierarchy of authority existed outside the
family but as an analogy with the family's structure: son respecting father, father respecting his father and the elders of the
tribe; those elders respecting the priests, who in their turn respect the high priest; and the high priest respecting God the
Eternal Father. So the pattern ascended from the example of the
home, for each father had to be a priest in his own home.

So too, in the New Testament Church, the hierarchy led from
each Christian home, where the father acted as shepherd over
his own sheep and lambs. Outside this fold were pastors and
bishops modeling themselves after "that great Shepherd of the
sheep" (Hebrews 13:20). But in each Christian home, as St. Paul
cautioned Timothy, should be found a husband-and-father who
is exemplary so far as his domestic life is concerned. As a matter
of fact, one of the qualifications stipulated by the Apostle Paul
for being a leader or overseer in the Church is that the candidate
"must manage his own family well and see that his children
obey him with proper respect." Then, as a parenthesis, St. Paul
adds this common-sense observation: "If anyone does not know
how to manage his own family, how can he take care of God's
church?" (I Timothy 3:4–5). Need I tell you, this Scripture was
always one of my father's favorite passages.

To us, as to the Israelites and Early Christians, this same command of Scripture goes out today. Every father must assume, as
his special gift from God, the responsibility to develop in each of
his children character through proper training and instruction.
Certainly, this is what the writer of the Letter to the Hebrews
intends when he uses the analogy of sons and fathers to explain
our relationship to God.

Endure hardship as discipline: God is treating you as sons.
For what son is not disciplined by his father? If you are not
disciplined (and everyone undergoes discipline), then you are
illegitimate children and not true sons. Moreover, we have all
had human fathers who disciplined us and we respected them
for it. How much more should we submit to the Father of our

spirits and live! Our fathers disciplined us for a little while as they thought best; but God disciplines us for our good, that we may share in his holiness. No discipline seems pleasant at the time, but painful. Later on, however, it produces a harvest of righteousness and peace for those who have been trained by it (Hebrews 12:7–11).

This is old-fashioned stuff, all this talk about discipline and character, not what you're likely to find in most of today's manuals on rearing children. It's increasingly popular among experts on "parenting" today to hold that mothers and fathers have no right to insist on a child's obedience, no right to discipline a child for rebelling and doing what he wants to do. In fact, some advocates of children's rights have redefined parental discipline as "child abuse" and are now proposing legislation that would remove a child from his parents' control if the child complains about being made to behave as his parents wish. Already in Sweden, a child may "divorce" his parents for the same reason. Talk about throwing out the baby with the bath-water! If such a time comes when the laws of our society forbid a father from disciplining his son—with all due concern for reasonable restraint —then we might as well go the rest of the way: Drive our children out into the streets and leave them there, as happens in the urban squalor of India and Bangladesh, Southeast Asia and Ethiopia. There an abandoned child, such as those homeless waifs one sees on the streets of Bombay or Chittagong, Bangkok or Addis Ababa, soon learns another discipline, the ways of the jungle and the survival of the fittest. Unloved, uncared for, such children spring up to adulthood like weeds in a vacant lot.

Of course, you don't have to go to the Third World to find this kind of tragedy in children's lives. Too many fathers right here at home are weaklings, afraid of their own children, afraid to lay down the law and let their sons and daughters know the rules by which they'll live. A scene from the movie *Kramer vs. Kramer* illustrates the modern father's ineptitude at requiring his six-year-old son to eat properly. Every word from the father only accelerates the little boy's disobedience. Not only are these fathers weak but also lazy. They don't have the tenacity to follow through with a child's behavior problem, preferring to let somebody else take over their job: teachers, pastors, traffic cops, social workers, parole officers. As a result, we're witnessing a new breed of disadvantaged children whose spineless fathers have allowed them to grow up with contempt for any other authority.

For instance, talk to most elementary school teachers today, and you'll hear them say that by all standards, children in their classrooms are more disrespectful, more unresponsive to authority, more undisciplined than ever before. "I spend most of my day," says Laura Fredericks, a sixth-grade teacher, "just in trying to control the class so that the few who want to learn can learn. It used to be that those of us teaching in grade school would hear the horror stories from high school; then the flagrant misbehavior filtered down to junior high. Now it's our kids who talk back, and some of them aren't at all bashful about telling a teacher where to go!"

School administrators aren't unaware of the problem today's lack of discipline at home engenders. They often complain that, when unruly children are brought to their attention and parents summoned to confront the issue, many parents refuse to acknowledge their part in providing an environment in which respect for others and self-control are taught. Bill Roberts, an elementary school principal nearby, reports, "All too often, in such a situation, parents just won't recognize any responsibility at all, or admit any weakness in their home. They try to put all the blame on the teacher. 'Why can't she control her class?' they ask. Or they resort to blaming some other kid for his bad influence on their perfect little saint. It's really disgusting to see grown men, especially, so weak, but there's almost nothing we can do about it."

Nobody sets out to raise a crop of crabgrass and nettles. But to obtain any fruitful harvest, we must plant the proper seed early in its season, then cultivate its growth into a healthy crop. You don't get tomatoes from dandelion seeds; you don't get giant baking spuds without hoeing the rows. So too with a child, especially if you're looking for that "harvest of righteousness and peace." It won't sprout up of its own accord, it won't appear from nowhere. If we expect to see the kind of fruit in our children's lives that brings us joy rather than sorrow, we must begin to work when they are young and continue, as long as they are in our care, to offer them training and instruction that lead to a disciplined character. In striving to achieve this happy harvest, each family needs the cooperation of both father and mother, working in unity of purpose toward the same goal. Admittedly, in our society this goal becomes harder and harder to achieve. What makes every parent's job today even more demanding is the way in which that job description seems to have changed.

For instance, under the old patterns the husband-father bore most of the burdens as provider, protector, and household policeman, as well as priest. According to traditional family structure, the man went out each day to earn whatever income his labor could produce; the woman stayed at home with her younger children while the older ones attended school. Her principal responsibilities lay in the domestic chores she performed on her family's behalf—cooking, cleaning, sewing, mending, washing, nursing, and caring for her family's emotional needs. When her husband returned home from his employment at sunset, he found his wife and children waiting to share the evening meal and the story of that day's events at home, at work, at school. If there were problems in the community or at home—threats to his family's safety or reports of disobedience on the part of the children—a father exercised his other responsibilities, to protect his family's welfare, to enforce the code of behavior expected of his children according to the moral and religious principles by which they were being reared. "Wait until your father gets home!" a mother might customarily warn her misbehaving son, and that boy would know he was due to receive punishment meted out by his father's stern hand.

Today, as we all know, there's increasing likelihood that no father at all is coming home after work. In Suffolk County on Long

Island, where I live, the divorce rate soared by 254 percent in the 1970s. According to the New York *Times*, the 1980 White House Conference on Families revealed that 45 percent of all children born in 1977 in the United States will live in a single-parent household at some time. Most of these households will be missing the father. Typically, therefore, a mother may be retrieving her youngster from a nursery school or an on-site day-care center where she works. Because of the number of children under public care, her child's discipline can only have been haphazard at best. Or she may be picking up her child at Grandma's or at a neighbor's house, where baby-sitting has consisted of turning on the television set for hours at a time. Now the child is in her care.

Because she's weary and, no matter how personally resourceful, burdened by the weight of being both mother and father, the last message any mother wishes to hear from those who care for her child is a detailed account of his naughtiness. Understandably, she chooses not to inquire; all too soon, she knows, she will probably have ample evidence of her own to deal with. Together mother and child arrive at their dwelling-place, and as evening begins, they attempt to interpolate into the chaos of their lives some sense of *home*. In those cases in which the mother is absent and the father has custody of the children, much the same sorry consequences of a shipwrecked marriage prevail.

Moreover, even in those marriages that still continue in blissful wedlock, the number of working wives now approaches a two-thirds majority in America. If a woman's place ever was exclusively in the home, rampant inflation and a runaway cost of living have forced that presumed ideal into oblivion. Very few middle-class families can afford the luxury of an unemployed wife-mother. As soon as possible after her childbearing has ended, the typical wife-mother resumes schooling to complete her education or training in some profession or skill and takes a job to augment her husband's income. For their part, few husbands, squeezed by this economic vise, can cling for long to whatever vision of themselves they may have brought into marriage—the breadwinner, his family's sole provider.

As a result of this obligatory change in the role of the man as his family's only provider, other role changes follow. If both father and mother are sharing the responsibility of income production, then they must also share in protecting and policing their family. Women, as much as men, must take on the duties of guarding their family's property and civil rights from unlawful intrusion or exploitation by thieves or "con" men, by government bureaucrats, by pollsters or credit analysts, or by undesirable religious proselytizers. It's foolish to keep one's wife in the dark about her husband's business affairs, his will and other legal documents. She needs to know about their investments, retirement plans, life insurance policies, securities, and debts. Husbands and wives together must exchange this information; fathers must be able to rely on mothers to do their share in protecting the family's interests, including the sanctity of the home.

Mothers as much as fathers must also accept shared responsibility for correcting their children's behavior. There may be valid reasons for delaying any major decision on punishment until consultation with the father; but a mother must not leave the whole court case for him to adjudicate and pass sentence. One reason why some children grow up to think of Mother as a weak flower and Father as a terrible ogre is simply that Mother has allowed her children to trample her without more than a murmured appeal to Father's eventual havoc-wreaking retribution. Like Zeus, he's expected to strike lightning bolts from afar! Arriving home from work tired and frustrated by it all, the last thing he wants to listen to are his wife's complaints about the children's disobedience. "Why don't *you* do something about it?" he asks. "Well, *you're* their father!" she replies, as if that privilege also named him as the Lord High Executioner. And so, to placate her—in spite of the fact that his judgment has been impaired by not witnessing the child's offense—he attempts to deal with the problem. He intends to be just and loving; more often than not, unfortunately, what the child receives is either another in a series of unfulfilled threats or else a spanking out of all proportion to his wrongdoing.

Henry Wadsworth Longfellow romanticized the family experience in his poem *The Children's Hour,* which begins,

> Between the dark and the daylight,
> When the night is beginning to lower,
> Comes a pause in the day's occupations,
> That is known as the Children's Hour.

But in many modern households that family reunion after work and school is a parody of Longfellow's ideal. Instead of children and parents coming together into *communion,* the family is torn apart by squabble, dissension, and quarrel, by angry accusation and rebuttal, by violent outbursts of physical punishment. How much better it would be, in a family of shared responsibilities, if each parent handled the problems as they arose and were encountered, using common sense and communicating with the other parent. How much better if a child grew up knowing not that Dad is the Final Authority but that Dad will support Mom's decision without undercutting her authority; that her express orders deserve the same respect as his. In many families today, the evening meal is the one occasion when most members can sit together at one time and recount to each other the day's happenings. For the sake of our digestion and nutrition—if not for reasons of tranquility and family order—this "pause in the day's occupations" must not be allowed to turn into a shark hunt.

But the main reason why a father's task, no less than a mother's, is the toughest job in the world is that it never ends. The challenges are daily, weekly, monthly, year after year. Being a parent is a full-time job with no reprieve, no time off even for illness and recuperation. Children, we soon discover, are *here to stay* for at least a score of years. They don't appear like robins in the spring, then fly away at summer's end; or if, as it sometimes seems, they do come and go during high school and college years, their absence in no way lessens our burden of responsibility. In fact, as our children get older, instead of relaxing, our task seemingly intensifies.

"It's the only job I know," says Ted Hutchens, a father with two daughters still at home and a son away at college, "that never seems to get any easier, in spite of all those years of experience.

"Our son Nathan comes home for Thanksgiving and wants to use the car on Friday night. He's a grown man, twenty years old; he's also a good driver. But, you know," he confesses, "Barb and I are wide awake, staring at the ceiling all night, until we hear that Oldsmobile come back into the garage. Then, because we're embarrassed to have him find us waiting up for him, we pretend to be asleep."

A father with three children in college understands Barbara and Ted Hutchens' situation. "I used to think that all the hard part was over," says George Mackey, "when they finally left for college. My wife and I thought we'd be able to sit back and take a rest from being parents. They were grown-ups, right? At least, that's the way they wanted it to be. My goodness, were we mistaken!

"When we took our first son to Middlebury College, he thought of ways to keep us from leaving him. He and his mother must have rearranged the furniture in his dormitory room six times before I finally figured out what he was up to. His sister, who went to Sweetbriar in Virginia, ran up telephone bills calling home like she owned stock in the company. She wasn't homesick, she insisted; she just wanted to make sure *we* weren't lonely.

"Now our youngest is away," George Mackey continues, "and he keeps us jumping with all his talk about taking time off to *find himself*. We'd like him to look in the mirror right where he is, at Rutgers, and see if he can find himself there. I tell you, it's more tiring being a father of college kids than it ever was when they were in the crib."

The point is clear: Once a parent, always a parent. Fathers and mothers alike, we don't stop caring just because we're no longer the main providers of shelter, food, and the comforts of home. It's not merely our bounden duty, as *The Book of Common Prayer* says, as biological parents of these children; it's also our joyful pleasure to care for them, even after they no longer seem to need us. This doesn't mean snooping on them, calling their college dorm or apartment at inconvenient hours just to check on their whereabouts. No father who has any reason to trust his son or daughter needs to behave like Shakespeare's Polonius, that wretched example of fatherhood in *Hamlet*. This old hypocrite piously mouths the creed of secular humanism:

> This above all: to thine own self be true,
> And it must follow, as the night the day,
> Thou canst not then be false to any man.

Then he promptly goes out and hires a private detective to report on his son Laertes, because it's in his nature to spy.

Sadly, a father who goes looking for trouble is rarely unsuccessful at finding it. What sends him on the prowl is an anxious suspicion that he hasn't done all he might have done to prevent trouble from occurring. He's not certain, after all, that he has taught his son or daughter the principles of discipline that produce character. I know a father much like Polonius in this respect. One evening, he excused himself from our living room, where he and his wife were among several couples Lory and I were entertaining. I took for granted that he'd gone to the bathroom; but no, when he returned several minutes later, he announced where he had spent the interim. Apparently knowing that one of our sons and his girl friend were watching television in my study, this peeping tom had crept to the study door, then burst into the room. What had he expected to find? I don't know for sure; all I know is what he said for himself: "You can do in your house what I'd never dare do in mine!" My response was intentionally curt: "That's your problem." His well-meant compliment fell flat, not only because of what it implied about his relationship with his own children but also because it insulted my relationship with mine. The fact is, I'd never think of sneaking up on my sons or daughter as if expecting to find them in a compromised situation. To do that would be to admit my total failure as a father by denying respect to my children.

At the same time, conscientious parents can't be stupid either. Our children, for all their training and instruction, inhabit a world hostile to those principles of discipline by which we've tried to shape their character. We don't sleep easily, oblivious to the temptations that haunt them, no matter their age. We must be responsive to the human condition and its frailty. So, as long as they come under our roof—or, to put it in utterly secular terms, as long as we claim them as dependents on our Form 1040—we have every right to inquire as to their whereabouts, their companions, and the nature of their activities. Our purpose isn't to pry; our expression of concern intends to remind both teenagers and young adults that we still care about them. Secretly, they welcome this fact, for it gives them security and a sense of well-being to know that, in a world of relative morality and evaporating standards, our expectations of them haven't changed. They can count on us to keep on caring, even though it's the toughest job in the world.

CHAPTER 4

A Sure Foundation

"The Child is father of the Man," wrote William Wordsworth. The poet meant that, if you want to see what a man will become, watch him develop as a child. The training and instruction that shape a child's character ordain what kind of man he is to be. So, if fathers want to develop in their children the kind of attitudes that will result in "a harvest of righteousness and peace," then they must make certain that the nurture they offer is indeed "the training and instruction *of the Lord*."

For fathers who really desire to give their children "the training and instruction of the Lord," their source of that *paideia* and *nouthesia* won't be Benjamin Spock or Haim Ginott but the teachings of Holy Scripture. In particular, the Book of Proverbs should be every father's guide to the successful nurturing of his children. For common-sense advice and diagrams of living situations, the wisdom of Solomon beats anything uttered by any child psychologist or reputed expert on "parenting."

The proverbs of Solomon son of David, king of Israel:
    for attaining wisdom and discipline;
    for understanding words of insight;
    for acquiring a disciplined and prudent life,
    doing what is right and just and fair;
    for giving prudence to the simple,
    knowledge and discretion to the young—
    let the wise listen and add to their learning,
    and let the discerning get guidance—

for understanding proverbs and parables,
the sayings and riddles of the wise.
The fear of the Lord is the beginning of knowledge,
but fools despise wisdom and discipline (Proverbs 1:1–7).

That's how the Book of Proverbs opens, and it's worth keeping
in mind the first principle implied for becoming a wise father:
You can't give what you haven't got. Before any "words of insight" can be spoken to sons, fathers must possess this same wisdom and discipline for themselves. Every boy loathes a phony,
especially if it's his own father. Not long ago, I overheard a student describing a quarrel between his parents. "My mom found
a copy of *Playboy* in my father's suitcase when he got home from
a sales convention. Was she mad!" He laughed at this, a little in-
sincerely, I thought; then, as he went on with his story, I knew
why. "Funny thing is, my old man had just been lecturing me
last weekend about how all the music I like to listen to is sex-
crazed. He kept telling me to get my mind up out of the gutter.
Well, I'd like to ask him where he keeps his mind, only I don't
have to!"

This boy's evident disappointment in his father is a lot more
common than many of us realize, and it's not an attitude restricted to sons alone. Writing in the New York *Times*, Gail
Sheehy tells of eight prominent women, including Rosalynn
Carter, Gloria Steinem, Phyllis Schlafly, and Bess Myerson, all of
whom seem to have adopted as adults ways of coping with their
childhood disappointment in their fathers. For instance, Sheehy
surmises, Jane Fonda's political activism is a reaction against her
father.

Shortly before Jane Fonda's 12th birthday, her father left the
family for what was described to Jane as "a trial separation."
Soon the father she loved was seen keeping company with a
girl barely out of her teens and asked his wife for a divorce.
Mrs. Fonda entered a mental institution. The cause of her
death shortly thereafter was kept from Jane until she read that
her mother had slit her own throat. . . . Jane Fonda has chan-

neled the anger at being betrayed when she was a powerless child into speaking out boldly on behalf of any group she sees as powerless.

How can we avoid making similar or worse mistakes as fathers? How can we prevent ourselves from creating resentment in our children? Only by obeying the Word of God and staking our lives on its truth. If indeed "the fear of the Lord is the beginning of knowledge," then before any father can dispense advice on "doing what is right and just and fair," he himself must know the meaning of that reverential awe and the wisdom to which it leads.

The goal of a father's godly instruction must be this spiritual insight called in Proverbs wisdom, knowledge, or understanding. But this wisdom isn't a scholastic accomplishment measured by high scores on the College Boards or admission to an Ivy League college. The true test of knowledge, according to Proverbs, goes beyond academic achievement to moral responsibility. It zeroes in on decision-making and shows itself best in the disciplining of the character; this results in "a disciplined and prudent life." To live prudently means to think clearly about one's choices and arrive at decisions controlled not by whim or appetite but by an understanding of the difference between right and wrong. This is what Proverbs also calls "discretion" or "discernment."

What we're talking about, then, is instruction that prepares a child to make wise choices, to be discreet and discerning. Such instruction doesn't presume that the child somehow already knows what's best. That kind of romanticism belongs to Jean Jacques Rousseau's theory of the "noble savage." Anyone who holds to a similar view hasn't spent much time around young children—say, in a nursery school playground, where children often show the very passions and violence that we shudder to hear reported on the evening news. Within the confines of swings-and-sandbox are all the components of theft, mugging, and murder, hinted at in the wrenching away of another child's toy, in a deliberate shove or kick, in an act of hateful anger by three-year-olds. As Adam's grandsons, such behavior is as natural to them as it was to Cain. So, from their earliest years, children must be taught and trained to tell the truth rather than lies; to respect the property of others rather than take for themselves; to keep from harming anyone else; to hold the miracle of life, whether animal, vegetable, or human life, in highest regard.

Yes, these lessons must be taught and then ingrained. They won't result from allowing a child to grow up in a moral vacuum, "doin' what comes naturally," as the song goes. Contrary to the views of certain psychologists, the moral nature of a child is not an untapped reservoir of innate goodness from which kind deeds will spring. Any boy or girl needs to be instructed in the fact that good and evil both exist, that right and wrong contend against each other, and that it's often difficult to choose to do right. Yet choose we must. "Decisions, decisions!" complains sixteen-year-old Connie. "It would be so much easier to live without having to make up my mind!"

Connie's desire to avoid the conflicts inherent in any dilemma is understandable, but it's also an indication of her immaturity, her lack of recognition of what it means to be a responsible and fulfilled human being. This power of choice she shuns is one of the founding principles of God's Creation. According to the Bible, God gives to the creature made in his own image a reflection of his own divine attribute called free will. In that freedom to choose, however, lies buried the risk of failure. Given the opportunity to choose, a human being may not necessarily choose wisely. Knowing this as mature adults, we may be terrified at the prospect of our child's apparent foolishness of choice. But that's the very risk God the Father accepts for himself. God could force us to obey him; instead, the Heavenly Father chooses to withhold his irresistible will. He prevents himself from compelling Man to love and obey him. With infinite patience, he waits for human beings to recognize God the Father for who he is; thereafter, adoration and obedience may follow—or may not! Rebellion may usurp God's authority, but that's a risk God is willing to assume in order to preserve the freedom of mankind to choose.

The same is true for human fathers and our children. We can't deny our sons and daughters their human right to choose; and so we must train them to accept the reality of living in a world largely determined by the choices they will make. Some of their choices will make us shudder, but if they're to reach maturity at all, we must be willing to allow them to fail. Perhaps in minor failures they'll learn to arrive at decisions more wisely, more prudently, without suffering the anguish of a major failure—their own or somebody else's.

The first and most important choice will be whether or not to pay attention to and learn from a father's godly instruction. From reading the Book of Proverbs, it seems apparent that the narrator-father knew the struggles his son would face in choosing between the father's counsel and the enticements of evil. This choice is never easy at any age—in the playpen, in the classroom, or in the family car—but in making his decision, to heed or not to heed his father's wisdom, a son must learn another biblical principle: the fact that choices have consequences.

We live in an era peculiarly ignorant of the relationship between *cause* and *effect;* in other words, many people seem ignorant that choices have consequences. In December 1979, persons in charge of a rock concert decided to sell "rush" tickets for a famous band; then they arranged with the arena management to open only two doors to admit the frenzied throng. Meanwhile, many in this crowd of young people were preparing for their evening's entertainment by indulging in drink and drugs; so that, when the doors of Cincinnati's Riverfront Arena opened for The Who concert, eleven people were trampled and suffocated in the melee. Why did these people die? Essentially because numerous individuals made bad decisions, unwise decisions, perhaps even immoral decisions, whose consequences led to these fatalities. Among the decision-makers were those whose ultimate choice might have been to avoid becoming part of the mob but who chose otherwise. In so choosing, they forged themselves as links in a chain from which there was to be no release.

Normal consequences may be either beneficial or unfavorable, profitable or disastrous. According to the narrator in Proverbs, beneficial consequences always result from making the right choice in heeding a father's advice, a mother's admonition. The Book of Proverbs overflows with such statements:

Listen, my son, to your father's instruction
    and do not forsake your mother's teaching.
They will be a garland to grace your head
    and a chain to adorn your neck (Proverbs 1:8–9).

Another passage describes how the narrator-father passes on to his sons what he had first learned from his own father:

Listen, my sons, to a father's instruction;
    pay attention and gain understanding.
I give you sound learning,
    so do not forsake my teaching.
When I was a boy in my father's house,
    still tender, and an only child of my mother,
he taught me and said,
    "Lay hold of my words with all your heart;
    keep my commands and you will live" (Proverbs 4:1–4).

But eventual disaster follows the deliberate choice to do wrong, as surely as *cause* determines *effect*:

The evil deeds of a wicked man ensnare him;
    the cords of his sin hold him fast.
He will die for lack of discipline,
    led astray by his own great folly (Proverbs 5:22–23).

Children, especially as they grow old enough to make such decisions for themselves, need to learn to anticipate the possible consequences of any decision. We face life with a positive attitude, expecting the best from prudent choices; otherwise, we'd be frozen in cataleptic fear of taking any action at all. But we must also be realistic about facing life and its unknown prospects; and while no one can read the future, we don't need to blunder on in total darkness either, not if we possess a discerning mind. Consciousness of cause and effect prevents anyone from being silly enough to suppose that he or she is immune from normal or abnormal consequences. Fire burns and water drowns, all the more if you're careless in dealing with these elements, and it does little good to swagger and say, "It can't happen to me!" Too many young people, dead at a lamentably early age, made the same boast. "There is a way that seems right to a man," says the narrator of Proverbs, "but in the end it leads to death" (Proverbs 14:12).

But the Bible promises to faithful fathers and obedient sons the joy of life. Indeed, this promise stems from the Fifth Commandment given by God to Moses, "Honor your father and your mother, so that you may live long in the land the Lord your God is giving you" (Exodus 20:12). Honor for parents begins with respect for the instruction they give to their children. The son who slights his father's teaching behaves like a bastard; the father who ignores his son's disrespect and allows him to make foolish choices without facing the consequences has already disinherited his child. Yet throughout our society the notion prevails that a father not only has no obligation but also no right to insist upon his son's behaving according to standards set by the father. The Bible declares quite the opposite and commands every father to instill in his son, by punishment if necessary, a sense of right and wrong and the need to choose between them wisely. As the narrator urges,

Do not withhold discipline from a child;
    if you punish him with the rod, he will not die.
Punish him with the rod
    and save his soul from death (Proverbs 23:13–14).

These are some of the principles that make up what St. Paul calls "the training and instruction of the Lord," discipline that leads to Christian character. But before going any further, two points need to be resolved. First, *discipline* must not be confused with *punishment*. Discipline may include punishment, but discipline is much more than just giving Peck's Bad Boy a hiding. To use an analogy from sports, an athlete's discipline is his entire training, never merely punishment. An athlete who refuses to let up on his calisthenics, who always strives to lift heavier weights today than yesterday, never runs at less than full speed, never allows time for an injured muscle to heal—such an athlete has a misguided notion about discipline and training. He's also being badly coached. Instead of training for excellence in performance, he's breaking his body apart in an exercise of masochism. The coach who, instead of disciplining his team, punishes them—like some notorious college and professional coaches in recent scandals—will reap a harvest of athletes who despise him and hate their sport.

The same is true of Marine Corps drill instructors, piano or ballet teachers, and fathers. While training must involve the strain of monotony and even the pain of having to correct one's faults, discipline is never an end in itself—which introduces the second point: Discipline leads to *self-discipline*. The whole object of disciplining a child's early development and growth to maturity is to establish an influence upon that child's eventual choices in later years. For, like the forms that hold concrete being poured into a foundation, a father's discipline serves only to stabilize and give shape to character until the time when it must stand alone.

The place to begin successfully disciplining children is with the father's own example. Like it or not, every father carries this enormous responsibility, to set an example worth imitating. Somebody has said, "Live so that your son, when people tell him that he reminds them of you, will stick out his chest, not his tongue!" Children are natural mimics; they ape the behavior of those around them, especially when that behavior identifies them with people whom they admire and wish to emulate. Children don't bother judging between right and wrong in the behavior they imitate; it's good enough for them to see that Daddy does it, and that makes it right.

A father took his eight-year-old son to the barbershop, and after each of them had had his hair cut, they stopped at the father's favorite local tavern for lunch. The bartender greeted his regular customer and said, "What'll it be, Mr. Thompson, the usual?"

"Yea, Joe, make it the usual," the father replied without thinking.

"What's 'the usual,' Daddy?" the eight-year-old inquired. "Can I have it too?"

Of course, there are privileges of adult behavior not granted to children. We don't need to apologize for our rights to keep later hours than our children or eat and drink in moderation what we forbid them. A licensed driver has privileges not belonging to an unlicensed adolescent; a married couple has privileges of intimacy not belonging to a teenaged boy and girl. But these privileges make us all the more responsible to carry them out in an exemplary manner. Our children learn from watching us, and they naturally assume that our behavior is acceptable as the norm for adults. So, if they see their parents habitually up late at night but slow to arise the next morning, our children will grow to believe that anyone can tilt the clock to suit his own schedule. But they'll have trouble understanding why the world expects them to be up and out the door to school while their parents lounge in bed.

Most of this disciplining by example will be unconscious on the part of both father and son. Neither will very often set out on any particular day to teach or learn from the other; instead, it happens spontaneously, in the day-by-day routine of living. If a man is careful about his personal appearance, he's teaching his son a whole series of lessons about cleanliness, neatness, and appropriate dress. While his son may not favor his father's hairstyle or cut of suit, the boy is learning daily that part of being a responsible adult means allowing time for personal hygiene and taking care to keep one's clothes in presentable condition. A friend used to go regularly through his son's closet, checking on the way the boy's clothes had been placed on hangers. From these inspections the boy received either a bonus or a fine on his weekly allowance. Similarly, if a man's a careless driver, impatient and reckless behind the wheel, he too is setting an example to his son. It will do little or no good to tell that boy, at age seventeen, to drive carefully. He'll drive the way his father's example has taught him, and only the strong arm of the law will compel him to learn otherwise.

There's no measuring the power of a good example. In his Prologue to *The Canterbury Tales,* Geoffrey Chaucer introduces us to the ideal clergyman, a pastor of whom the poet says,

> This noble ensample to his sheep he gave,
> That first he wrought, and afterward he taught.

In other words, the priest practiced what he preached; by his life he illustrated in advance what he later expounded from the pulpit. For fathers no less than ministers, the rubric is the same, as Benjamin Franklin wrote in *Poor Richard's Almanack,* "A good Example is the best Sermon."

But what a tragedy when a father's behavior exemplifies hypocrisy and falseness rather than sincerity and truth, like Shakespeare's Polonius. Here another character in literature comes to mind, Willy Loman in Arthur Miller's American classic play, *Death of a Salesman.* His sons are Biff and Hap, now in their thirties; one, a ne'er-do-well who moves from job to job without purpose or fulfillment; the other, a sensualist without a moral scruple to his name. We meet these men, father and sons, on the last two days of Willy's life, when his despair mounts to suicide. What causes this despair? Willy has failed to succeed as either a salesman or a father. His first failure he might have survived, lying to his wife about the business of selling merchandise throughout New England, fudging his faltering commissions by borrowing enough from a neighbor to pay his insurance. But the second and larger failure is mirrored in the moral vagrancy of the two grown men who are, in every respect, their father's sons.

This failure cannot be endured. The question this play asks can be summed up in these words: In a family so manifestly committed to what one son calls "the old honor and comradeship," how is such a collapse possible?

We find Arthur Miller's answers to this question represented by the disparity between Willy's pronouncements on ethics and his personal examples of immorality. In his troubled mind, wracked by unacknowledged guilt and recrimination, Willy Loman reenacts his sons' teenage years, carried back in time by hallucination and reverie. Now once again, Biff is seventeen, a senior in high school, a football star and romancer of young girls; Hap lives in his older brother's shadow. Upon Willy's return from a sales trip, his sons seem to wait upon every word of his accomplishments: how many gross he sold, which mayor he met, which sports hero's autograph he's brought home to them. It all seems perfectly innocent and adoring—a man's sons looking up with pride at their father. But appearances are far different from reality, for in conversation with his equally adoring wife Linda, Willy confesses some of the truth. He's exaggerated greatly his earnings to impress his family; in fact, his sales are nowhere near his quota. He no longer possesses either his confidence in himself or the smooth charm by which he sets such store.

Willy Loman is a study in personal contradictions. When his sons greet their father, Willy praises Biff's "initiative" in stealing a football; then, to impress his own older brother Ben, Willy sends his sons across the street to a construction site to steal some lumber. Yet in a moment of anguish, Willy asks himself about Biff, "Why is he stealing? What did I tell him? I never in my life told him anything but decent things." To Willy's discredit, he neglects the importance of teaching by positive example. It hasn't been enough merely to *tell* his boys how to succeed in business. He ought to have been *showing* his sons how to live a decent life. For the whole truth is that Willy is a philanderer, a womanizer with an illicit relationship in every city throughout his territory. At the height of his personal crisis in the play, Willy

Loman relives his lowest moment: Biff's discovery of his father's infidelity in a Boston hotel room.

After this catastrophe—Miller tells us through another character—Biff gives up on himself. At age seventeen, Biff's spirit dies when his father, his idol, crumbles before him. He becomes a wanderer, a lost soul. His younger brother Hap, for his part, determines to carry out Willy Loman's dream. With that decision, the audience knows, Hap also seals his fate because his father's dream has been nothing more than an empty illusion based upon deception and lies.

Each of us is human, subject to those frailties that are the consequences of sin. All too soon our admiring sons will discover that we too have feet of clay, that we're also susceptible to error, just as capable as anyone else of committing grievous mistakes. Two things, therefore, every father must learn in determining to set a wholesome example for his children. First, a father must humble himself and admit that he can't be the ultimate and faultless example; he can only serve to reflect the image of a higher Example for his sons and daughters to follow. Second, a father must be quick to acknowledge when he has been wrong, and then seek his children's forgiveness. This may be a father's highest example of Christian virtue; it may also be the hardest for him to attain.

I've told this story before elsewhere, but it bears repeating here. Our family spent the summer of 1971 in Oneonta, New York, living in a rented house while Lory took graduate courses at the State University there. We had Elsa, our highly independent cat, along for the summer. Several times she'd expressed her dissatisfaction with her temporary accommodations and gone off for long periods, and I was concerned about getting her back home to Stony Brook. On the day that Lory's studies ended, we cleaned the house and packed our station wagon with the summer's luggage. Throughout that final morning, I kept on sounding the warning of what would happen to anyone whose carelessness might let the cat get loose. I knew—as I somehow felt nobody else was capable of knowing—how inconvenienced we would be if Elsa took off for the day. A couple of times, one or another of the children left the screen door ajar by mistake, and I pounced upon the cat just before she made her getaway. Such evidence of everyone else's thoughtlessness confirmed my sense of personal superiority; thus enraged, I berated them all with increasingly horrible imaginings of the fate awaiting the culprit who let the cat escape.

That culprit—as you've undoubtedly guessed—turned out to be me. When everyone was settled in the Plymouth Fury wagon, I carried Elsa to the car and smugly placed her on the front seat, then slid in and slammed the door. Next stop Stony Brook. But the sound of the door scared the cat. She scrambled toward the back of the station wagon and sprang out the open tailgate window I'd neglected to close.

What happened over the next few minutes—and stretched into diabolic hours of anger—makes me ashamed even to type these words. I'd been so sure of myself, so ugly in threatening reprisals against the person who might let the cat get away; now I had to face up to what my threats meant. Short of hara-kiri, I could think of no real punishment that would fit my crime. Not wishing to accept that sentence of death, I couldn't accept living with my own wretchedness either. In rage at myself, all perspective vanished, all focus became blurred. The only thing on my mind was how foolish I must appear to my children and wife. But instead of acknowledging that foolishness and asking forgiveness, I compounded its folly by indulging in recriminations against myself and everyone else. I'd tasted the bitterness of self-hatred; now I was spreading its poison around me.

Lory must have been praying for grace because we retrieved the cat almost right away. But it took me several hours to recover my senses. Just before reaching the George Washington Bridge, we pulled over at a fast-food outlet. As we got out of the car—making very certain this time that Elsa was safely stowed—I found the words to ask for pardon. Forgiveness washed by tears and blessed by laughter made those frankfurters the best I've ever eaten! When we got back into the car to continue our journey home, Ellyn said to me, "Elsa forgives you too, Daddy."

It's too bad how often our behavior makes our children weep. "Why is it," a young woman in seminary asks me, "that my father's so unyielding, so incapable of acknowledging a mistake? I'm twenty-two years old, and I've never once heard him say, to my mother or any member of the family, 'I'm sorry.' He's a good man, an earnest Christian, an elder in our church, but he just can't face up to the fact that he's human.

"I love him," she goes on, "but I'd love him so much more if he'd just accept himself for who he is and stop pretending to be infallible."

Accepting ourselves for who we are: That's a necessary step in establishing healthy relationships with anyone else—wife or husband, brother or sister, parents or children. We have to learn not only to love life, protecting ourselves in response to natural urges of self-preservation, but also to *like ourselves*—to place a high value on our very existence, to grant ourselves the esteem we deserve. Unless we care about our own lives and our worth as persons, we can't very well express much interest or concern in the personhood of anybody else. But where does such self-esteem— our proper sense of importance as persons—come from? And how does our being who we are affect our relationships with others?

That source of personal worth is the God who made each one of us. Because he's our Heavenly Father, Creator of heaven and earth and all things visible and invisible, he deserves our worship. Nothing created in love by God can be treated with contempt or indifference, because its very being calls forth expressions of approval from the Creator-Father. Since each of his creatures is precious to him, they also deserve our respect. Loving God, therefore, begins not with solemn prayers and ritual but with acts of love for his creation; for it is through "deeds of love and mercy," as the hymn writer Ernest Warburton Shurtleff says, that "the heav'nly kingdom comes." Loving God means recognizing the worth of what he has chosen to create; loving God means accepting our responsibilities to care for his creation—

including other human beings made, like ourselves, in the Father's image. This is what Jesus pointed out when he declared the Great Commandments:

"The most important one," answered Jesus, "is this:
'Hear, O Israel, the Lord our God, the Lord is one. Love the Lord your God with all your heart and with all your soul and with all your mind and with all your strength.'
The second is this: 'Love your neighbor as yourself.'
There is no commandment greater than these" (Mark 12:29–31).

But how are we to love God and love our neighbor until, first, we've learned to love ourselves? That's the problem facing many pious people. They've been taught, from early childhood, to accept the theological fact of innate depravity, their own especially. They've read the self-accusation of St. Paul, calling himself "the chief sinner." They've sung the hymns of John Newton and Isaac Watts, in which the singer describes himself as "a wretch like me" and "such a worm as I." It seems perfectly appropriate, in light of such humility among saints and sages, to think of oneself in the lowest possible terms. But what's true about me, the thinking goes, must also be true about you—my wife, our children, our other relatives, our neighbors and casual acquaintances. This means that none of us is any better than the next person. We're all worthless slime.

But just the opposite is true! Yes, as rebels against God's divine authority, we've been judged worthy of divine condemnation; yes, there's nothing good enough about us to raise ourselves out of the quagmire of our own sinful pride and disobedience. But even so, *we matter to God.* He loves us so much that he refuses to allow us to remain in our degraded condition. He gives us his very own Son to be the offering for sin, the means of redemption that buys us back from the devil's pawnshop and restores us to full standing with God the Father. If God loves us that much—and he does!—then we ought to recognize and rejoice in our own inestimable worth as persons. I must love myself because only then am I able to love you in the same manner and to the same degree. When I love my neighbor *as myself*, then self-preservation changes to brotherhood: I care enough about my life to fight to the death to save your life too. When you trip and skin your knee, my bones ache and my flesh bleeds too. Furthermore, when I fail to live up to my responsibilities, when I fall short of being the kind of loving neighbor both God and you expect me to be, it hurts you just as much as it hurts God and me. Our relationship is reciprocal, an even flowing of love and joy, pain and sorrow—either and both—between us.

Nowhere does this exchange of love mean so much as in the family relationship. Husband and wife loving each other as one caring for each other's needs, not *as though* but *because* her needs are my own needs; parent and child sharing gain and loss as joint partners; all of us together living in full realization that the best proof to demonstrate that we love God is this: We treat each other with that same caring concern we yearn to receive ourselves. Jesus summed it up in these famous words: "Do to others as you would have them do to you" (Luke 6:31). This means that, if fathers and mothers expect their sons and daughters to honor their parents, to offer them respect and dutiful obedience, then parents must acknowledge their responsibilities to honor and respect their children as persons. This means, from time to time, eating humble pie and learning to say, "Forgive me, kids. I've been a fool." Erich Segal, author of the novel *Love Story*, is wrong when he defines love as "never having to say you're sorry." Genuine love, the only kind of love that counts, is just the opposite.

It takes courage to accept ourselves for who we are, to say "I'm sorry." It takes courage to love ourselves enough to offer that same love to others. Why? Because such love runs the risk of failure. Every father, every mother, knows this fear. Yet it's a risk we must take if we are to fulfill our responsibilities to our children. We have to be willing to sacrifice our pride—even, if necessary, our status as parents—for the sake of love's larger good.

Let me share another story with you. I've always been proud of my role as a parent, father of the family, head of the house. I've taken my responsibilities seriously, but along with those responsibilities I've claimed certain privileges reserved for elders—what Edward Gibbon called "the insolent prerogatives of primogeniture." But as our children have grown older, it hasn't always been easy to know how best to handle their struggles to assert themselves and claim their own rights as persons. Sometimes I think I'm protecting an ever-diminishing territory as a threatened sovereign.

Take, for example, the matter of the family automobiles. Recently, when our sons and daughter have all been home during the summers of their college years, use of these cars has been an occasional cause of misunderstanding and even strife. An old Mustang, good for local shopping trips and not much more, and a newer LTD, possessing both air conditioning and a stereo tape deck, became the objects of conflicting interests. Not that these cars themselves were ever really at issue; no, what we sometimes disputed were property rights and responsibilities as family members. To me as the household patriarch, the argument seemed clear: Our adult earnings had bought both cars; we licensed, insured, and when necessary repaired them, also with our earnings. Both were registered in my name as the owner of record. Therefore, when either mother or father wished to use a car, it must be available to us—clean, fully serviced, ready to go. Because we're a family, not a corporation, I didn't feel we needed any formal requisitioning of the car; I certainly didn't charge our children so many cents per mile. I simply expected us to live by a mutual understanding of who has prior claim: ME!

We reached a point one summer when I began to wonder if my name had been changed to Hertz. It seemed that the cars were seldom available when I needed one of them. Too much was being assumed about the younger drivers' rights with too little corresponding responsibility in return. Nothing major, you understand. A trip to the ocean had to be delayed, for instance, not only because the last driver had brought the LTD home gasping for gas but also because nobody in recent memory had bothered to check the oil or the tires—or the battery or the fan belt, or anything more than the supply of cassette tapes. A showdown seemed inevitable, and it occurred the next weekend. Don and Kevin had planned to drive 600 miles round trip in the August heat. Obviously, the Mustang wasn't the proper vehicle for such a journey. Knowing that I also needed a reliable car for a preaching engagement that weekend, my sons arranged to borrow a friend's car for me to use, while they took the air-conditioned, stereo-bedecked LTD. But this same friend was accompanying them on the trip; so why not ride in his car? Why swap my LTD for his Datsun?

Many angry thoughts must have been seething under the surface that summer because they all came exploding upon us in this trifling crisis. In particular, Kevin and I had an unusually incendiary outburst. At first, like a cloud of steam from an overheated radiator, our words obscured the real issue between us. Accusations and denials, sarcastic judgments made in anger, tough talk countered by tougher talk. Finally, it was all too much for Lory, who screamed at us both, "I can't stand this any more! Get out of this house!" So we did, taking our quarrel outside to the redwood furniture under the trees. There something happened. Perhaps in the expanse of a summer noonday—our grievances with each other no longer able to bounce off the kitchen walls—we gained some emotional distance from our problem with each other. Suddenly, we found ourselves in tears and hugging each other. We'd both come simultaneously to a realization that neither of us was right and the other wrong; we were both wrong, yet trying to defend a hopeless position. My pique at having someone else's car pawned off on me, at having my authority as the owner of the LTD usurped, weren't important in themselves. Kevin's rage at my apparent selfishness wasn't the point either. At stake was only this: Does my excessive pride cancel out his irresponsibility?

Of course, I could have continued to stand my ground, asserting my spiritual rights as head of the family, my legal rights as New York State's official owner of the car. But I knew very well that I'd lose far more than I could ever gain. Once I faced myself with this fact—and Kevin came independently to his own insight —the only reasonable action was for each of us to yield to the other. I bandaged my hurt pride and dissolved its selfish appearance; for his part, without rancor Kevin offered to cancel the trip. At that point, I could have claimed a Pyrrhic victory. By giving up nothing more than a few words of apology, I'd gained full possession of my car for the weekend. But that too would have been an empty triumph.

A few hours later, when both boys had come home from work, I met them and said, "I'm sure we could all have handled this business and ourselves more like Christians, with greater consideration for everyone else's needs." They agreed, and I went on: "I'm sorry for letting my pride turn to selfishness, and I'm certain you are both sorry too." They looked at each other and back at me, nodding in acknowledgment. "Here are the keys to the LTD. Drive safely, and have a good time."

Both boys were flabbergasted at my concession; I might add, I was too. They hadn't expected it, and their appreciation has been evident ever since. Weak? Spineless of me? I don't accept those charges. There's such a thing as wanting to be right for its own sake; there's also the desire to be right for Christ's sake. Any father can bully his sons and daughters, but it takes more strength than any of us can claim to possess—it takes the strength of Jesus Christ's love—to lead our children by seeking their forgiveness instead of wallowing in our own bitterness and pride.

Every father lives with the quiet desperation of knowing, on the one hand, that he needs to be an example to his children; on the other, that his shortcomings disqualify him from being a model of perfection. That's why, in the long run, a sincere and honest father points beyond himself to show his family the examples offered by God the Father and God the Son. In two passages from Paul's letters we have the Bible's most direct statements regarding their divine example:

> Be imitators of God, therefore, as dearly loved children (Ephesians 5:1).

Then this beautiful declaration:

> If you have any encouragement from being united with Christ, if any comfort from his love, if any fellowship with the Spirit, if any tenderness and compassion, then make my joy complete by being like-minded, having the same love, being one in spirit and purpose. Do nothing out of selfish ambition or vain conceit, but in humility consider others better than yourselves. Each of you should look not only to your own interests, but also to the interests of others. Your attitude should be the same as that of Christ Jesus:
>
> > Who, being in very nature God,
> > > did not consider equality with God something
> > > > to be grasped,
> > but made himself nothing,
> > > taking the very nature of a servant,
> > > being made in human likeness.
> > And being found in appearance as a man,
> > > he humbled himself
> > > and became obedient to death—
> > > > even death on a cross! (Philippians 2:1-8).

The record of Jesus of Nazareth's life and teachings, found in the Four Gospels, shows us by what standard we ought to live. He was subject both to his earthly parents and to his Heavenly Father's will. The man Jesus never lost sight of his relationship with Mary and Joseph—living in obedience to them as a child, expressing concern for his mother's care and protection even in his own dying anguish—because this too was part of doing his Father's business. In turn, his mother Mary and guardian Joseph came to recognize that Jesus wasn't their private property, that he was a child of promise belonging to the Most High God. "Do whatever he tells you," Mary instructs the servants at the wedding feast (John 2:5). Jesus Christ is the perfect Son, and in him we also come to know his Father; as he told Philip, "Anyone who has seen me has seen the Father" (John 14:9).

From living in the light of these examples of leadership with humility, every man can learn to say, again with St. Paul, "That is why, for Christ's sake, I delight in weaknesses, in insults, in hardships, in persecutions, in difficulties. For when I am weak, then I am strong" (2 Corinthians 12:10). When a father takes God the Father as his example and clothes himself in the humility of Jesus Christ, he can look another human being in the eye, even someone as close to him as his own son, and say with confidence, "Follow me. Do not only what I *say;* do as I *do!"*

CHAPTER 5

Setting the Standard

"You know what's tough about being a father?" a friend I sometimes run with asks me as we pant through a six-mile workout. "Knowing the difference between being a pal and being the boss."

Dick Wittman, the father of my godson Richard, is right, and many a man would agree with him. Knowing where to draw the line between familiarity and respect, knowing when to advise and when to demand, knowing how to keep the roles of father and son distinct from each other so that each may serve the other's needs—that's a hard maneuver to manage, especially today, when fatherhood is under attack as an outdated convention of male domination.

A man whose own boyhood has been essentially happy wants to give his son the same kind of relationship he enjoyed with his father; conversely, a man who suffered through an unhappy youth naturally looks to establish a different kind of relationship with his own son. Larry is a case in point. "I never knew my father—or any of my mother's other husbands," he says. "She had four or five; I sort of lost track because most of them left me alone. My father just took off when I was about two, and the other men didn't stay around for long either." Larry's mother was a career woman who spent a lot of time traveling. "When she wasn't married, she took me with her. When she was, she sent me off to boarding schools and summer camps. You might say that the men I learned most from were hotel desk clerks and bellhops."

Larry's son David certainly can never complain that he was abandoned by either his father or mother. They swarmed all over him with love and attention. Larry had been an outstanding athlete, close to making the Olympic swimming team, and he worked with his son from the time he could creep and crawl to develop his interest in sports. But not to the neglect of his mind, for Larry had overcome his spotty schooling to earn a Ph.D. in ancient history and classics. Both he and his wife Nan, a college literature teacher, spent long periods teaching David to read before he was four years old. Larry certainly had the prizes to show for his efforts. David excelled at everything he tried in school and in sports. At each grade level he scored off the scale, pushing our local schools to their limits in challenging his mind. He won the punt-pass-and-kick contest and was actually banned from pitching in organized sandlot baseball because he threw too fast. David went with his father to several scholarly conferences overseas, where Larry had been invited to read a paper. In other words, by the time he was ten, the boy had seen the world and claimed it as his own.

Of course, Larry insisted that his wife and he be on a first-name basis with their son. It was always Larry and Nan and David, never "Daddy" and "Mommy" and "David." After all, weren't they equals? They did everything together, and as David entered his teens, Larry became more and more like an older brother. His hair was as long as David's, and they wore the same costume: work shirts, jeans, and boots. When David began having difficulty with school authorities because of various dress codes or other regulations, his parents took him out of school altogether; they tried tutoring him themselves, then turned to correspondence courses through a university extension. With no school team participation, David's interest in sports declined; it was replaced by playing an electric guitar, which would have been fine if he'd been willing to take lessons. But David preferred to teach himself by imitating the recordings he played day and night.

About this time, Larry's wife began to realize that something was seriously awry in her son's experience. She tried to convince Larry that some changes were needed in David's life. But Larry couldn't be convinced, and David misread his mother's concern for betrayal and oppression. At fourteen, he left home and went to California's communes. Larry refused to pursue him, a decision that led to Nan's divorcing him. Larry next heard of David's whereabouts when he saw his son's face in a newspaper photograph of a crowd at a Rolling Stones concert. Today, in his early twenties, David works on an assembly line in an airplane factory. He writes to his father occasionally, but he hasn't been in his father's house in years.

"It hasn't been easy, seeing David turn out to be less than I'd hoped for him," says Larry. "But I can't go through the rest of my life asking myself where I went wrong. I did the best I could; I gave him everything I never had as a kid. I kept him from a lot of silly pressures, like getting a haircut just so you can play on the varsity team. I let him have the freedom to make his own decisions. I'd probably do it all over again, just the same way."

Doug's childhood was quite different from Larry's. Doug's father was a tyrant, a minor league Napoleon who kept his wife and only son under total submission to his egomania. He supposed himself to be right on all issues, never allowed a question or a contradiction, especially on matters of religious concern. In time, his narrow-mindedness led him to form his own congregation, separate from all other groups of Christians. As Doug himself describes his home life, his father insisted on the most spartan kind of existence, although his income could have provided much more comfort for his family. Of love and affection within the home, there was scarcely a word spoken or a gesture made. Christmas and the celebration of birthdays were considered pagan observations unworthy of a Christian home; so Doug grew up without knowing most of the pleasures common to other boys.

"I felt so starved for love as a kid," he says, "that when I became a father, I just wanted to pour out of myself all the love I never found from my own father."

And he did! By the time Lory and I came to know Doug and his wife Ruth, their son Junior was about three, a bright and curious child who could hold a conversation with any adult in the room. But with children his own age, it was a different story. By age nine or ten, Junior knew more about electronics than anyone other than his father; he was aware of politics and mortgages and income tax, matters completely foreign to most boys his age. He knew—or seemed to know—every intricacy of the family's financial planning, carrying with him his father's concerns about vast economic crises and ecological disasters that only a Ralph Nader could ponder. He was his father's bowling partner and fishing companion, but increasingly Junior was also the person with whom Doug went to the movies. There was no rating system in those days, but the movies Junior saw with his father rarely would have earned a "PG" by today's standards. When our sons were still hoping to see "The Million-Dollar Duck," Junior and his father had reviewed several films whose themes were considerably more mature.

"It was a way of opening up a conversation," Doug says. "If the action in the movie was over his head, I thought he'd ignore it; if it interested him, he'd talk about it."

By the beginning of sixth grade, Junior had lived what little boyhood his father had allowed him. He'd been rushed into adolescence and on toward adulthood to serve his father's need for a pal, a confidant. At twelve, he was a somber-faced old man living in a little boy's body. He had friends, yes, but none of his schoolmates claimed to understand him. He spoke a different language from theirs, his speech an echo of his father's worries and concerns. Throughout high school, Junior became more and more withdrawn from his own age group. As his social life constricted, so his handwriting shrank to a microscopic scrawl and his conversation became terse and infrequent. Neighbors began to report seeing him walking the streets long after midnight. His parents shrugged off their evident dismay when Junior next an-

nounced that he wouldn't be going to college, as they'd expected. Instead, he was heading for the Maine woods to work his
own hours, responsible to no one but himself. "That's Junior,"
they said. "He's always been his own man."

Junior came home not long ago and announced that he's been
living with an older woman for the past year or so. Maybe they'll
get married, maybe they won't, but he just wanted his folks to
know. His parents understand that this news isn't the end of the
world, but it nonetheless tears away at something deep inside,
especially for Doug, who wonders why.

What went wrong for Larry and Doug? Somehow both these
fathers missed their cue. They came onstage to play the wrong
parts. Each wanted some other role than what God had called
him to be—a *father;* not a dictator or a bully, but not a brother
either. Their earnestness in following the wrong course, their sincerity, makes their confusion all the more painful, for both these
men are dedicated Christians who pray for God's best for their
sons and themselves. Yet, somehow, these men never learned
that a child needs someone to tell as well as show him what's
right and what's wrong. That someone must be loving and
strong, patient and firm, hopeful yet true to the realities of
human experience; that someone must be a father. He can't be
just a buddy; besides, a boy will pick and choose his own bud-
dies among boys his own age. The role a father assumes calls on
him to take charge of shaping his son's character. This means
that in the father-and-son relationship, there's not much room for
discussion among equals; it's not a democratic forum. It's a moral
gymnasium where the father trains his son for life's most rigorous challenges.

Sometimes, however, the roles do reverse, if only temporarily.
A child becomes the teacher, a parent the pupil. In my own case,
I've never been much of an outdoorsman; in fact, I never even
earned my Cub Scout merit badge for camping. But a few years
ago, my sons signed us up to join a group of fathers and sons
from our church on a canoe trip through Algonquin Park in Ontario. Don and Kevin both had far more experience than I from

various expeditions they'd taken with school, church, or summer camp. In spite of my reluctance to expose myself as a novice camper, they convinced me to take time away from the typewriter and see the world from a new angle.

We were gone for ten days, carrying our food and shelter on our backs, fighting off mosquitoes the size of DC-10s, making two dozen portages, enduring lashing rain and leaking tents and swamping canoes. One afternoon, Kevin caught the seat of my pants with an errant fishing hook. Another time, Don rebuked my paddling, and we had angry words over who belonged in the stern. There were some other low moments along the way; but even though I was a tenderfoot among Indian scouts and braves, I learned to enjoy the quiet splendor of that northern wilderness, its clear water sipped from a paddle blade, its crystal-cold nights. I saw myself removed from the confidence of familiar surroundings, taking advice and learning from my sons. I remember vividly the morning, on one of the last portages, when I was finally able to pick up our canoe, hoist it over my head, and with my pack bear it for some 600 yards, all the time singing at the top of my voice,

> Must I be carried to the skies
> On flowery beds of ease . . .

If my sons hadn't insisted, I'd never have been able to claim my share of God's riches in nature. I'd never have known this dimension of my boys' character or profited from their example. In the woods and on the lakes I was in their classroom, and they taught me from their experience.

Whatever his own boyhood has been, there is a standard by which a Christian father can bring up his son, a fixed point of reference by which to gauge our lives. That standard may be found in God's Word. We've already seen the Bible's warning to fathers, to pass on to their children's children the Law of God. It's repeated in Deuteronomy, in Proverbs, in the New Testament letters. But now it's necessary to say a word of caution and assert the importance of making sure that what's passed on from generation to generation really is a standard of divinely inspired, biblical morality, not just a cultural or social preference. There's a world of difference between these two. One standard is absolute, the other relative. One carries with it the force of God's decree; the other has only the weight of conventional behavior and social ethics.

According to God's absolute decree, as given to us by St. Paul, "all have sinned and fall short of the glory of God" (Romans 3:23). Without exception, all human faults are a result of the presence of sin in human beings. Whatever virtues exist are an evidence of God's common grace to every individual, preventing us from being as wicked as we might choose to be. In spite of our sinful nature, God insists on showing us just a silhouette of what we can become through the special grace of Jesus Christ's redemption. But it's sin that makes us unloving when we want to be loving; sin that makes a sham of the so-called "Christmas spirit" we yearn to preserve for just a moment more of peace on earth, goodwill to men. Sin is rebellion against God. A bumper sticker seen on the Long Island Expressway last summer spoke these frightening words: RESIST ALL AUTHORITY. That's the motto of anarchy, the denial of any sovereignty other than our own. Anarchy is the religion of the ego, the inordinate desire to be my own boss, to rule the universe.

Since this is our natural state, the condition in which we're born, it's commonplace to say, "Nobody's perfect," and that's true. It's also true that everybody is estranged from God, separated from his promised life, alienated from every facet of his perfection. That's the description St. Paul uses in his letters to the Ephesians and Colossians. But Paul is speaking in the past tense of a condition no longer true:

> Once you were alienated from God and were enemies in your minds because of your evil behavior (Colossians 1:21).

What's made the difference? The fact that forgiveness is possible and aliens can become citizens; so Paul says:

> Remember that at that time you were separate from Christ, excluded from citizenship in Israel and foreigners to the cove-

nants of promise, without hope and without God in the world. But now in Christ Jesus you who once were far away have been brought near through the blood of Christ (Ephesians 2:12–13).

Forgiveness brings with it reconciliation, a restored relationship with God. But this restoration comes about only by acknowledging one's sin, seeking repentance, accepting forgiveness, making restitution, and avoiding a repetition of the same sin. Here's the pattern set forth by King David in his great penitential prayer, recorded as Psalm 51. David acknowledges that his sin—adultery with Bathsheba and the murder of Uriah her husband—is always in the forefront of his mind: "For I know my transgressions, and my sin is always before me" (Psalm 51:3). He asks for cleansing and an assurance of God's forgiveness in verse 12: "Restore to me the joy of your salvation." But since he can't give back Uriah his life, he offers to do the next best thing—to be an example of righteous living to others and so deter them from sin: "Then I will teach transgressors your ways, and sinners will turn back to you" (verse 13). In place of ritualistic sacrifice, the repentant king offers "a broken and contrite heart" (verse 17), which he's certain that God will not disdain to accept. In time, David knows, he will again offer the sacrifice of the righteous, but not until he has once more proved himself faithful to God.

I love the prayers by which I am summoned to confess my sins and receive God's pardon. *The Book of Common Prayer* says, first,

Ye who do truly and earnestly repent you of your sins, and are in love and charity with your neighbors, and intend to lead a new life, following the commandments of God, and walking henceforth in his holy ways: Draw near with faith, and make your confession to Almighty God, devoutly kneeling.

Then on my knees I join with other worshipers—my wife, our daughter and sons—in this great prayer of confession:

Almighty God, Father of our Lord Jesus Christ,
maker of all things, judge of all men:
We acknowledge and bewail our manifold sins and wick-
edness,
which we from time to time most grievously have committed,
by thought, word, and deed, against thy divine Majesty,
provoking most justly thy wrath and indignation against us.
We do earnestly repent,
and are heartily sorry for these our misdoings;
the remembrance of them is grievous unto us,
the burden of them is intolerable.
Have mercy upon us, have mercy upon us, most merciful Father;
for thy Son our Lord Jesus Christ's sake,
forgive us all that is past;
and grant that we may ever hereafter
serve and please thee in newness of life,
to the honor and glory of thy Name;
through Jesus Christ our Lord. Amen.

After we've prayed this prayer, my parish priest offers this assurance of forgiveness:

Almighty God, our heavenly Father, who of his great mercy
hath promised forgiveness of sins to all those who with hearty
repentance and true faith turn unto him, have mercy upon
you, pardon and deliver you from all your sins, confirm and
strengthen you in all goodness, and bring you to everlasting
life; through Jesus Christ our Lord. Amen.

This too is old-fashioned—sin and repentance, forgiveness and
restitution. These aren't the common terms of today's popular
psychology with its saccharine slogans touting everybody's
healthy-mindedness and freedom from guilt and repression. But
the Bible says quite otherwise, and so we've got to decide, as fathers, which to believe. If we intend to give our children "the
training and instruction of the Lord," we need to guard against

allowing ourselves or anyone else to impose *non*-biblical standards upon our children. *Non*-biblical standards are the ways of the world, whose origin is the Serpent's lie in Eden, contradicting God's command and reinterpreting God's plan for human happiness. We encounter that same lie today in the casual suggestion that since "everybody's doing it," that's sufficient warrant to make such behavior acceptable for us too; or in a relative morality that finds any excuse, any cause for equivocation, to allow for disobedience to God's Word. Usually that equivocation tries to juggle the irreconcilable differences between "human values" and God's Law. The result, predictably, is always in favor of "human values," even when they fly in the face of what the Bible teaches. Whenever this happens—whenever the commands of God through Scripture are ignored or twisted to satisfy our own justification—that's *sin*, plain and simple. The Apostle James says it bluntly: "Anyone, then, who knows the good he ought to do and doesn't do it, sins" (James 4:17).

But *extra*-biblical standards are also contrary to the Bible's teaching because they present themselves as a means of attaining a higher state of grace than faith in Jesus Christ already offers. By not dancing, not drinking, not smoking, not attending the movies, and so on down a changing and often inconsistent list of no-no's, a Christian can guarantee himself membership in the First Church of the Circumcision, in suburban Galatia, where this error started. And it *is* error because, you see, either the sacrifice made by Jesus Christ is sufficient to redeem us from sin and restore us to fellowship with God the Father, or it isn't. If he is sufficient, anything else we do as believers we do only because we love him, not because we feel the need to add to our redemption what Christ has been unable to supply. If he isn't sufficient, then it stands to reason that nothing we can do can make up for his inadequacy; indeed, the whole business of trying for a relationship with God on even terms becomes preposterous anyway, so why bother? In either case, getting yourself circumcised, whether physically or symbolically by a system of legalistic constraints, is a waste of effort. But St. Paul has the best word on this matter in a verse I seldom hear as a Sunday morning text: "As for those agitators, I wish they would go the whole way and emasculate themselves!" (Galatians 5:12)

Children from Christian homes are facing increased challenges from both *non*-biblical and *extra*-biblical codes of behavior. In both cases, pressures to conform crowd in upon them. From those who scoff at the thought of God and his place in human affairs, the pressure may be overt or subtle, bullying or snide. For the child it may mean the hurt of feeling left out of school or community activities, clubs or teams. Social pressures will undoubtedly call upon the parent to be patient, wise, and gracious in explaining why, for instance, your son or daughter can't regularly miss Sunday School and worship services in order to play in the Sunday morning soccer league. When you explain, make sure your reasons are solidly grounded in the Bible's teaching about the Lord's Day and Christian worship. Likewise, your reasons must be biblical for not permitting your child to attend a birthday party at which the principal entertainment will be playing with a Ouija board; or a beach party at which the main events are cocaine sniffing and sex in the sand dunes.

But witchcraft, drugs, and casual sex aren't the only predators upon youth today. Even within the Christian community at large —especially the evangelical subculture with its schools and colleges, clubs, and summer camps, as well as local churches—there are increasing pressures to conform to particular codes of ethics. These strictures, sometimes stated but often only implied, call for pledges and promises and personal commitments to abstain from this or that activity of which the subculture disapproves. By its very selectivity of censurable behavior, such a list often glamorizes certain practices and makes them more attractive than they need be. It also fails to treat the root of the matter, preferring to specify the sins of the flesh but making little mention of envy, gossip, spite, or any of the other sins considered to be less lurid, less embarrassing to the institution.

Consider dancing, for instance. When I was growing up in the 1940s, and '50s, my father and his fundamentalist Baptist churches forbade me from going to dances at school or at private parties. Of course, dances weren't the only entertainment disallowed by my spiritual mentors; also *verboten* were the movies, ice shows, bowling if there was a bar on the premises, and any form of Sunday sports. My parents took a more liberal view than most regarding the theatre, not only permitting but encouraging me to see live drama onstage. But, as I say, this contradiction was unusual in our church confederacy, and we didn't talk about it to the congregation.

The rule against dancing, however, was taken for granted. No one in my father's congregation known to frequent the dance hall would be fit to teach Sunday School or sing in the choir or serve on the board of deacons. This restriction carried over into our school experience, as you might imagine. In physical education classes, I joined with friends from our church or other churches of similar persuasion in presenting our teachers with requests from our pastors, excusing us from dance instruction and participation on grounds of conscience. This was largely ironic for me because my conscience wasn't troubled at all. What troubled me was this: What was so special about dancing that my church and pastor (often, but not always, my father) wanted to keep me from it? Somehow I reckoned that it must have to do with the fact that the people we might have danced with were *girls*. Since I was already shy about any dealings with the opposite sex, at first I wasn't really terribly dismayed to be kept from holding them in my arms and spinning around the floor in time to the music. But in time that shyness changed to curiosity, and with it I discovered why dancing was taboo: It stimulated inordinate sexual desire! Or so I was told. But this too baffled me since sexual desire was a burden I already carried without benefit of knowing a waltz from a lindy. Nobody in my church, or at home, for that matter, had much to say regarding that problem. More on this topic later; right now, it's enough to say the obvious: I never learned how to dance. More important, I never really learned *why*, at least not in terms supported by *what the Bible teaches*.

As it turns out, my fundamentalist tutors, who inveighed so

loudly and so long against the dance in all its forms and modes, were almost right but for the wrong reason—which is frequently more detrimental than being altogether wrong. Basically, dancing is a response to natural rhythm. Swaying, clapping, stomping, and similar body motions are the free expression of that response. It's a tribute to our humanity, to the wholeness of our being, that causes us to react rhythmically to the pulsation of our emotions.

Careful study of the Bible often reveals that its own statements about a matter offer a more balanced view than the particular teaching of those with some axe to grind or some special doctrine to promote. By the imbalance they create, these zealots in fact lead to distortion and perversion of biblical teaching. Certainly this is true in the conflict between those who consider dancing to be inherently evil and those who see that the Bible teaches something quite different. Admittedly, the apostate Israelites, after erecting the golden calf, danced themselves into a licentious frenzy; admittedly, John the Baptist lost his life because King Herod became infatuated with a belly dancer. But is this all the Bible says about dancing? Certainly not.

Dancing is also an expression of praise to God (Psalms 30:11, 149:3, 150:4; Jeremiah 31:13), as demonstrated when King David "danced before the Lord with all his might, while he and the entire house of Israel brought up the ark of the Lord with shouts and the sound of trumpets" (2 Samuel 6:14–15). The absence of dancing signifies sorrow or even rejection by God (Ecclesiastes 3:4; Lamentations 5:15). In one dramatic instance, an objection to dancing spotlights the mean spirit and jealousy of one man for another.

Meanwhile, the older son was in the field. When he came near the house, he heard music and dancing. So he called one of the servants and asked him what was going on. "Your brother has come," he replied, "and your father has killed the fatted calf because he has him back safe and sound." The brother became angry and refused to go in (Luke 15:25–28).

Literal-minded fundamentalists, who pride themselves on their obedience to every word of Scripture, need to ask why the Prodigal Son's father calls for dancing as part of the celebration of his son's return—and what the Elder Brother's refusal to dance means in the parable's interpretation!

Yes, dancers can be stimulated to erotic desires, and why not? They were meant to be. Among many species of God's creatures, male and female engage in a dance of some description. For instance, certain kinds of hunting spiders go through contortions to display their brightly colored bodies to prospective mates. Male web-spinning spiders also dance, vibrating a strand of the female's web in such a way as to attract her attention as a mate rather than as potential prey. Peacocks display their gorgeous tail feathers, and the dominant rooster in the coop parades as the "cock of the walk." For each of these creatures of nature, the dance is part of courtship, a sacred prelude to mating or copulation, and so to procreation, in fulfillment of God's command to multiply. Likewise for human beings in every tribe and culture, the dance is both a social phenomenon and a sacrament of human sexuality anticipating union in the partnership called marriage. But by the very fact that the dance represents something holy, the dance is also in danger of being defiled and corrupted by lust: for only that which already bears the marks of sanctity can become debased by sin.

Last weekend, Lory and I attended a wedding and the joyous celebration that followed. The bride is Greek, and her father provided musicians at the reception whose music called forth rhythms even from my stone feet. The bride and groom led us in a symbolic waltz. Their parents followed; then came the other members of the bridal party. Finally we all joined them, signifying by our participation in the union of the dance a holiness and sanctity to the occasion. By our act of clasping each other in the formality of dance, we were saying to the bride and groom, "We approve of your union in marriage. We celebrate with joy the love that brings you together, a love that will produce children as the fruit of your marriage."

Here's the beautiful and holy truth about the dance. By its choice of partners and their orderly and graceful movement together, it symbolizes what God has ordained to be the most essential element of human experience, the relationship between man and woman in marriage. This relationship, in turn, represents the love expressed by God for his Creation, made known to us in the Bible as the marriage between Christ and his Church. Precisely for this reason, dancing shouldn't be compromised and cheapened by the decadence of "Saturday Night Fever" and Studio 54's disco orgy. But why was I kept from learning the whole truth about dancing? Why, during my years of teenage development, instead of being made to feel guilty and depraved, wasn't I taught by my Sunday School teacher or pastor or father to know and heed *what the Bible says* about dancing and other amusements? The answer is that these well-meaning adults, blindfolded by their church's definition and fear of "worldliness," couldn't see for themselves. They'd been conditioned by the negative preaching of those who could only tell what's wrong with the dance.

Much the same argument might have been made here concerning the conflict between total abstainers and those who drink in moderation. I've chosen to talk at length here about dancing only to make this point: The negative teaching I received, concentrating solely on the evils of dancing and attending the movies and other taboos held up by my religious subculture, ran counter to biblical standards for Christian growth toward maturity. Negative teaching, by its index of prohibitions, narrowed my Christian development by presupposing that the natural human response to music and rhythm is essentially dangerous and should be suppressed. Its whole attitude toward human experience told me how frightened Christians must be of their own bodies—which is why we heard so many sermons about becoming more "spiritual." My fundamentalist upbringing (and such teaching still goes on) is as close to the heresy of gnosticism as any superorthodoxy can be. Gnosticism, which plagued the Church as early as the days when the Apostle John wrote his letters, claimed that all material things are evil in essence; hence, Jesus of Nazareth could not be God-in-flesh. But this teaching itself is refuted by Scripture, and in its place we're told to rejoice in the fact that we've been made in the same flesh and blood, the same form and substance, as that in which God chose to manifest himself as the Incarnate Lord. We're to exult in the fact of being human, with human bodies; we're to accept ourselves without fear. For, as Paul said to Timothy, "God did not give us a spirit of timidity, but a spirit of power, of love, and of self-discipline" (2 Timothy 1:7). Once more we find that the real purpose of Christian nurture is preparation for self-discipline, not merely the adhering to a set of rules and regulations imposed and policed by some outside authority

The evangelical subculture can be a hotbox for Christian young people, especially when family or institutional pride is at stake. Christian parents will naturally be cautious about protecting the family's name, the family's reputation, and as members in good standing these parents will carefully supervise their children's spiritual growth. When our children are young, we may find it convenient to keep them in line by compelling them to meet the common standards of the family and the church we attend. "Everybody in this house goes to Sunday School," we may say to a suddenly reluctant five-year-old; or we may appeal to the child's sense of pleasing his teacher: "Poor Miss Emery! She'll be so disappointed if you're not there!" For a while our children will accept an edict like, "A Robinson doesn't lie!" or "Nobody in this family smokes; it's a dirty habit." But as these children grow older, family pride as such may have to be reexamined in the light of developing personal values. Over the years, a son may have seen and never forgotten an occasion when his father or some other pillar of the church fell short of the prescribed standard. As an individual the child begins to question whether or not the family's do's and don't's make sense to him. Are they valid? What's the real source of their authority? Only the strongest voice in the family or the personage behind the pulpit? Or is there, perhaps, some higher law to be obeyed?

Your local church, your denomination, your Christian school or college can set up any arbitrary code of ethics it wishes. For example, it can ban the wearing of toupees or watching TV's "Masterpiece Theatre," but how much nearer the Kingdom of Heaven will its members be for all that? To establish any other standard than what the Bible itself declares scandalizes the Gospel and discourages teenagers from discovering the real meaning of Good News. When I was a teenager in Brooklyn, New York, one of my friends was another preacher's son named Harmon. His father was the pastor of Salem Gospel Tabernacle, a Scandinavian Assemblies of God congregation where they knew about the presence of the Holy Spirit long before the word "charismatic" became a slogan. It was the early 1950s, and Harmon and I sang regularly in a quartet at a Saturday night youth rally in downtown Brooklyn. We weren't especially good singers, but we had what every quartet needs—a uniform. We wore matching teal blue suits made with the then-fashionable long lapels and tapered trousers; if I'm not mistaken, we also wore chartreuse ties! One Saturday afternoon, Harmon didn't show up for rehearsal, and he wasn't there to sing that evening either. On Monday, when I saw him next, he explained his absence: One of the elders in his father's church had "lost the victory" over Harmon's pegged pants and complained to the pastor. Not wishing his son to give further offense, Harmon's father restricted him from singing with the quartet as long as we wore our zoot suits. But since none of the rest of us felt convicted of having caused a weaker brother to stumble, we just replaced Harmon with another second tenor and went on singing, pegged pants and all.

Who gained and who lost in that encounter? All that can be said about the aggrieved elder is that any grown man who can "lose the victory" so easily over a teenager's apparel must be living on the edge of defeat most of the time. As for father and son, I know only that, after being forced to quit the quartet, my friend Harmon became disheartened and rebellious, wandering a long way from his father's House of Peace. Thank God, in time he came back to acknowledge the reality of Jesus Christ in his life. But the folly of the case is plain: As fathers, we have to realize that God is less easily offended by our children's features than we are because, as the Lord told Samuel, God isn't impressed by fashion or physique. "Man looks at the outward appearance, but the Lord looks at the heart" (1 Samuel 16:7).

No, family pride and conformity to institutional standards—whether the church's ethics or the school's code—won't do. We've got to beware of the insidious teaching that causes our children to think that, by maintaining the subculture's standards for approved behavior, they've met the higher standards of biblical morality. It ain't necessarily so! Obviously, it's perfectly possible to go through childhood and adolescence—as many young people do—without once defying either parental or ecclesiastical taboos. For example, to this day I've never smoked a cigarette; I've done a lot of other things of which neither my father nor his Baptist churches would approve, but smoking isn't one of them. Under a legalistic code, I might reasonably have convinced myself that just because "I don't smoke, and I don't chew, and I don't go with the girls who do," I'm on my way to heaven. There's a real danger in setting up any artificial standard of morality which, when achieved, becomes an end in itself. Why do you suppose so many people, when asked about their relationship to God, speak not of faith in Jesus Christ but of all the bad deeds they avoid and all the good works they can lay claim to?

Christian fathers, we have to learn to focus on what's really taught as biblical truth and not permit our vision to be deflected by extraneous matters. As for *what's really taught,* we can find it in various contexts such as the Ten Commandments, the Sermon on the Mount, the Great Commandments ("Love the Lord . . . and love your neighbor"), and various admonitions in the apostles' letters. Our sons and daughters need to come into close acquaintance with what the Bible itself says about right and wrong, truth and falsehood; they need to learn that the great Christian virtues are faith, hope, and love, "but the greatest of these is love" (1 Corinthians 13:13). They need to know the difference between what St. Paul calls "the acts of the sinful nature" and "the fruit of the Spirit." Sin shows itself in "sexual immorality, impurity and debauchery; idolatry and witchcraft; hatred, discord, jealousy, fits of rage, selfish ambition, dissensions, factions and envy; drunkenness, orgies, and the like. . . . But the fruit of the Spirit is love, joy, peace, patience, kindness, goodness, faithfulness, gentleness and self-control" (Galatians 5:19–23).

CHAPTER 6

The Point of Balance

"But if we don't have a clearly defined set of standards," someone may say, "how will our sons and daughters know right from wrong? Won't they run wild if we don't hold up a barrier against sin?" This is a genuinely serious question and deserves a thoughtful response. For our common ground we have to agree that the Christian father's goal is to train his son for a life of spiritual maturity after that son has left his father's household. The Bible teaches that self-discipline, self-control, and moderation are the proof of this maturity; these virtues come from striking a balance between freedom and responsibility.

One of Jesus Christ's promises to his followers is that the Holy Spirit will be our Counselor. "When he comes," says Jesus, "he will convict the world of guilt in regard to sin and righteousness and judgment" (John 16:8). In other words, it's the job of the Holy Spirit, living in us as Christians, to discriminate between sin and righteousness, to judge between the two. But on what basis do we judge? Well, we can use the catalogue of vices and virtues enumerated by Paul to the Galatians. Sexual immorality and adultery are the opposite of real love, debauchery is the opposite of authentic joy, discord of peace, and so on. These are obvious. Fornication, getting drunk and smashing up a party, spreading rumors that cause hurt to other people are all clearly sinful. But what about other human actions that seem to be neutral, like playing the piano or playing basketball? Certainly they *are* neutral; there's nothing morally good or bad about the keyboard or the backboard. But if your son spends hour after hour working on chords and arpeggios, if your son spends all his time shooting jump shots, to the neglect of school work, household chores, church activities, and other responsibilities, then that teenager's life is out of balance, so much so that a potentially good thing comes dangerously close to being sinful.

To recover the balance, your son needs the power of the Holy Spirit working through you to help him discern for himself and judge between the right use of his time and the wrong. For make sure you know the difference! It isn't playing the piano or playing the sport that's wrong; it's the abuse of time spent out of proportion to other important tasks. The presence and power of the Holy Spirit in a believer's life acts like a thermostat to control the balance between extremes of hot and cold, license and inhibition. Finding and maintaining that point of balance means coming to understand what St. Paul says,

> "Everything is permissible for me"—but not everything is beneficial. "Everything is permissible for me"—but I will not be mastered by anything (1 Corinthians 6:12).

When a Christian achieves this balance, it brings true *liberty*, the freedom to live responsibly and abundantly in the new life offered by Jesus Christ. There can be no higher standard.

But precisely because that standard is so high, we must be reasonable in our expectations. Frank A. Clark has said, "A father is a man who expects his son to be as good a man as he meant to be." Clark's irony stings, for all of us know its truth. How easily we forget what it means to be a child! We need to recognize the difference between outright disobedience and the normal stages of immaturity. We've all heard a father say to his son, "Act your age!" We look around, expecting to see him talking to an adult dressed in a banker's suit; instead, we find a kid in dungarees and a polo shirt, with a runny nose and a world of wonder in his eyes. Whatever he's doing that annoys his father, one thing is certain: He's probably acting his age! What his father has demanded is quite absurd. He wants the little boy to act *his* age—to behave like a thirty-five-year-old executive, very polished in speech and manners.

Or another situation. Six-year-old Danny takes a bad spill off his bicycle. He runs screaming to his house, looking for comfort and relief from the pain of his skinned knee. He meets his father and, sobbing, shows his wounds, but instead of comforting him and taking the pain to himself, his father says, "Come on, Danny, big boys don't cry." But Danny isn't a big boy; he's a little boy who hurts. Furthermore, his father isn't telling the truth. Big boys do cry, or ought to. Perhaps if Danny's father cried a little more often—that is, felt and expressed some measure of human compassion—Danny's home might be a more completely humane place to live.

We must define and refine our understanding of disobedience so as not to confuse children by requiring the impossible, then holding them accountable for performing our demands. It's an old adage that a child must walk before he runs. We teach children the alphabet, then two- and three-letter words before we expect them to read and pronounce polysyllabic monstrosities like *antidisestablishmentarianism*. We teach our sons to play baseball with an oversized bat and a large spongy ball, knowing that the time will come when they must use a regulation Louisville Slugger and a Spalding horsehide. But for the time being, we waive the rules. For these beginners it isn't "three-strikes-and-you're-out!" We recognize how hard it is for them, coordinating vision and muscle control, to hit the ball, and so we throw pitch after pitch until they can match Ty Cobb. Then we start bearing down and calling balls and strikes.

We modify our expectations of children in their mental and physical development until they've reached an age when they can justifiably be held accountable for knowing how to read and spell, how to add and subtract, how to ride a bicycle safely, how to take a telephone message accurately. That's just good sense on our part, and we wouldn't dream of doing otherwise. But we need to do the same thing, modifying our moral and spiritual expectations of our children, just as God the Father has done toward us because of our frailty. The Psalmist tells us,

The Lord is compassionate and gracious,
    slow to anger, abounding in love. . . .
He does not treat us as our sins deserve
    or repay us according to our iniquities. . . .
As a father has compassion on his children,
    so the Lord has compassion on those who fear him;
for he knows how we are formed,
    he remembers that we are dust (Psalm 103:8, 10, 13–14).

Not all fathers are as gracious as God is. I once observed a teacher who systematically penalized his pupils for scratching out a word or two and writing in a revision; he also required each student to cut the eraser off the end of his pencil. When asked about his absurd demands for perfectionism, the teacher defended his position with the remark that he expected his students to think before they wrote, and thereafter to write correctly. He could not be convinced that revision itself is a valid form of thoughtful composing, and that erasing to start over is an act of intellectual humility worthy of commendation rather than rebuke. You won't be surprised to learn that this same teacher treated his young son and daughter with similarly categorical firmness. I remember in distress the terror of his daughter's scream when, one evening at the dinner table, she happened to spill a glass of milk. One would have to think long and hard to find a crime for which the punishment she received might be deserved! Fortunately for his students, this twisted personality was fired as a teacher; unfortunately, he could not be fired as a father.

While visiting in another home one evening, my wife and I were invited to share in the parents' bedtime devotions with their two children, both preschoolers. The father held the children on his lap and began reading to them—I could hardly believe it!—from an adult commentary on the Lord's Prayer. Words like "petition" and "recompense" drifted overhead. Before very long, both children had advanced from restless squirming to energetic striving to get free from their father's grasp. But for whatever reasons, he held them more tightly and read on and on, pausing only to rebuke first one, then the other, for interrupting. Whom was he trying to impress? When the reading was finally over, then it was time for questions and answers. Of course, the young children had nothing to contribute, for all their father's earnest priming for response. Their mother, a reasonably sensible woman, tried her best to get her husband to end the embarrassment to us all, but this debacle came to its own conclusion when the father, having lost all patience, excused himself and grabbed the older child to head for another room. There the inevitable happened, a spanking better deserved by the father than his child.

We train up a child in the way he should go in the same manner that we climb a great mountain or complete a long journey: one step at a time. To rush ahead and demand more than a child knows how to give isn't only foolish but also destructive to that child's will to please. For we must begin by acknowledging that it's on the basis of pleasing his father and mother that a child first learns to obey. The poet Wordsworth claimed that each child came into this life with innate knowledge gained from some previous existence, so that birth was, he said, "a sleep and a forgetting" of that prenatal intelligence:

> Not in entire forgetfulness,
> And not in utter nakedness,
> But trailing clouds of glory do we come
> From God, who is our home.

A romantic suggestion, indeed! Not one, however, supported by a biblical theology of man's creation by God, man's subsequent fall from grace, and the resulting doctrine of innate depravity. Rather, a child comes into being as a creature whose will is already bent against any other authority than *self*. The child knows and cares nothing about moral law or the Ten Commandments; he knows nothing except that when he is hungry, he wants to eat; when he is wet and uncomfortable, he wants his diaper changed; when he is tired, he wants to sleep. But this child learns quickly how to attract his parents' attention, and before long he can also tell, by the difference between one tone of voice and another or the difference between tenderness and rough handling, what pleases and displeases. He learns to perform little circus acts in response to a doting father's silly questions: "How big is Billy? So-o-o-o BIG!" And the baby laughs.

Why does he play this game? Because the baby perceives, however dimly, that it pleases his father and creates an environment of joy; conversely, when he spits out his formula or pouts over being set down, the infant knows that his behavior causes the climate to become tense and threatening. So he learns to accommodate to his mother's wishes, his father's pleasure, and this becomes his means of distinguishing right from wrong. He judges after the fact, by consequences, and he learns to repeat those conditions which, in the past, have led to pleasant results. Every infant is a pragmatist; he judges good from bad on the basis of what occurs as a result of his action. Not until much later does a child come slowly to understand that there is another dimension to good and bad besides what pleases Daddy. Beyond the level of immediate consequences and reaching into the very core of moral concern, this knowledge unveils to the child a dimension of spiritual reality in which sin and righteousness, judged by God's standards, must be differentiated. Now the child's objective changes from pleasing parents to satisfying a holy God's demands for righteous living. The child hears and learns from his father what the Bible says is right and wrong:

> He has showed you, O man, what is good.
> And what does the Lord require of you?
> To act justly and to love mercy
> and to walk humbly with your God (Micah 6:8).

Eventually, however, the day arrives when the child can speak his own mind and say the single word of rebellious self-assertion: "No!" That's when conscious correction begins, countermanding the child's expressed willfulness with loving insistence. Yes, he will remain seated in his high chair and not crawl all over the family table. No, he will not throw his bowl of strained prunes and chopped liver on the floor. And if he refuses to eat the nourishing food offered at mealtimes, he will not be allowed to nibble or nosh between meals. No, he will not be expected, at age two, to sit quietly during an hour-long worship service; but by age four, he will have begun to recognize and respect his father's demands for stillness during what is called "prayer." By age eight or so, he will be able to sing and read along with the rest of the congregation, and by twelve or fourteen, he should also be able to retain some of the pastor's sermon and discuss it with his father and mother during Sunday dinner.

An unusual child may reach these various levels of maturity sooner than others, but comparisons aren't important. Even Jesus himself wasn't discussing theology much before the age of twelve; so we certainly shouldn't despair if our children don't appear to be terribly excited by arguments over the authorship of the Letter to the Hebrews. What counts is this: Are they learning to live by the simplest rudiments of God's Law? Do they tell the truth? Do they show respect for other people's rights and property? Do they honor their parents' authority? Do they know that God's Name is holy and not to be cheapened by curse or casual use? It's unrealistic to expect too much too soon, and the penalty for parents making this mistake is our children's frustration and discouragement.

But this doesn't mean that our expectations remain limited, frozen at a level of childish capacity. Our teaching, our disciplining, must be progressive and developmental. Intellectually and physically we don't remain at the level of monosyllables and easily lobbed pitches. As we begin to stretch our child's mental and physical proportions, so we expand our moral and spiritual expectations, making our demands more challenging. This means that we mark our child's advance toward maturity by giving him an ever-broadening range of opportunities to show that he's growing up, that he can handle greater responsibility. As he moves from infant to toddler, from preschooler to kindergartner, from Little Leaguer to jayvee and then varsity letterman, from boy soprano to baritone, his privileges and responsibilities must also grow. With growth come changes in our goals and expectations.

I believe in letting children know what they can look forward to in the way of new privileges, along with our expectations; then holding strictly but sensibly to that timetable. For instance, with two sons just one and one-half years apart in age, it was sometimes difficult to give one privileges on the basis of age, while restricting the other. In fact, in some instances we made no distinction at all; both went away to summer camp at the same time, and both began piano lessons simultaneously. But at age twelve, Don received permission to go by train with Danny Dodd, his best friend, to New York City—just the two of them—and spend a day sight-seeing. Kevin, who had just turned eleven, wasn't included, and I'll never forget how badly his nose was out of joint that day. It was his older brother's first great adventure, and Kevin was acutely conscious of having been left out. But to mute his disappointment, I suggested that he invite two or three friends his age to go on their own excursion. A day or two later, this foursome of fifth graders hopped on board the Long Island Railroad for their one-stop ride to Port Jefferson, the end of the line. It wasn't the length of the trip that mattered; it was the fact that they did it all by themselves, just like the older boys. Port Jefferson offered only limited fascination for Kevin and his friends, and so after stopping at a diner for a piece of pie, he phoned home; I drove the six miles over and picked them up. But from the smiles on their faces, you'd have thought that their journey had been epochal. Well, in a way it was! It served to tell them and the rest of the world that, while these younger boys weren't yet of an age to take on The Big Apple, like their somewhat older brothers, nonetheless their parents trusted them enough to let them out of the nest.

Sometimes it's easier for parents to make these decisions about expanded privileges by relying on support from legal restrictions, such as when the law declares one may or may not obtain a driver's license. Obviously, no parent can decide to grant driving privileges to a child two or three years under age; parents too are subject to the law's higher authority. But the time comes when an adolescent reaches the eligible age. What to do then? Well, *then* isn't the time to begin considering the proper decision. A child doesn't suddenly arrive at sixteen or seventeen with no previous training in the responsibilities of caring for life and property. Parents ought to be watching carefully throughout the early teenage years and offering the needed correction and discipline that brings a child to young adulthood.

When that time comes, parents must make clear to their teenagers the difference between privilege and right. No citizen has any inherent right to a driver's license; it's a credential earned by evidence of the ability to drive carefully and responsibly. It can be suspended or revoked by the same powers that granted it. But long before that driver's license has been stamped with a young person's name, his parents should be exercising their own "road tests." There may be no direct parallel, but if a person is careless about certain important areas of his life—if he tends toward procrastination and is always trying to make up for lost time by rushing—what does this trait suggest about the way he will drive his car? What guarantee can the teenager offer that his misplaced sense of responsibilities in school, work, or home affairs will suddenly be set straight when he gets into an eight thousand dollar sedan?

Mutual trust is the desired and desirable point of balance between father and son. Children want to be, *need* to be, trusted; their personal sense of worth thrives on knowing that their parents believe in them. They crave opportunities to show themselves worthy of our trust. "I can do it, Dad. I'm old enough!" pleads a youngster eager for a chance to prove himself. But nothing damages a son's spirit quite like his father's refusal to believe in him. The father who opens his son's mail or lifts an extension telephone somewhere in the house to tap his son's conversations does permanent harm to their relationship. You can't conduct your family's business like a ring of secret agents, with nobody quite knowing friends from enemies. If a father has some uneasiness about his son's correspondence, he should ask to be shown the letters that trouble him. If the letters are above reproach, the father will need to explain to his son why he suspected otherwise and then clear the air between them with an earnest apology. If the letters confirm the father's fears, then he will deal with that problem directly, without the added burden of having to defend his own underhandedness. That's the least any son has a right to expect from his dad.

Above all, our expectations should be expressed as briefly and as simply as possible. Our wishes don't need to be as complicated as an insurance policy. A child should know and be able to recall without question or doubt what his parents expect of him in a given situation. In our family, my wife and I always tried to keep our rules to just these four statements:

1. If it's right, enjoy.
2. If it's wrong, you know what to do.
3. If you're in doubt, then you know it's wrong.
4. Always—no matter what time of night—*always* telephone if you're going to be later than we expect.

Lockerbie's Laws don't cover every human possibility, but this little list has served well enough to get our three young people to voting age and beyond without major calamity to them or lasting trauma to us. I recommend something similar for you and your family.

But even something as simple and straightforward as these few rules can't guarantee that sons and daughters will always be obedient. Of course they won't. They too are human, subject to that same willfulness and pride that leads us to sin; they're no more invulnerable than we are. So we must remain realistic about our children's behavior, praying for their spiritual fortitude but prepared for each of them to stub his toe and fall. Indeed, we should be willing to allow them to fall because it's part of our joy to help them back on their feet, forgiven and ready to continue their pilgrimage with Jesus Christ. When he falls—and he will—a son must find his father resisting the natural desire to stand back and smugly condemn. Recrimination or accusation after the fact resolves nothing. "I told you not to hang around that crowd!" "I warned you what would happen if you spend all your time listening to that trash!" This is no more than nagging.

My rector, Canon Paul F. Wancura, tells the story of a father who took his young son to church one Sunday morning. Apparently, the boy was, first, inattentive to the service; then, bored by it all, he fell asleep. Following the service, the father and son went to a restaurant and sat in a booth next to one occupied by a woman who had also been present at the same church. From the time the pair were seated, the father began berating his son for his behavior.

"How could you be so immature? Why couldn't you sit quietly? Have you no respect? And to fall asleep . . ." His tirade continued throughout the meal, making it impossible for the woman in the next booth not to overhear. The effect of the father's barrage obliterated any appetite she might have had, and she was certain that neither man nor boy could possibly be enjoying his meal.

Rather than continue, she pushed aside her plate, stood up and turned toward her fellow-parishioners. "Oh, how nice to see the two of you!" Each of them mumbled some pleasantry, hoping she would leave without further embarrassing them, but she lingered to say, "I don't quite know what's wrong with me today. I'm just so restless, I haven't even been able to finish my meal. You know, it all started in church this morning. I just couldn't seem to concentrate on the service, and then the strangest thing happened: I actually fell asleep during part of the sermon. Well, I must be going. Nice to see you."

The story isn't meant to justify a child's disruptive or irreverent behavior; but by looking closely, we can see how the woman's technique may have been more effective than the father's in establishing the fact that the boy's behavior—like her own—was unacceptable. When we aren't satisfied, we need to say so, insist upon a change of behavior and attitude, hold up a standard of improvement the next time, and leave it there. Nagging is the most counter-productive instrument of discipline. Because it's almost wholly negative, nagging seldom works. Consider: How much benefit does a nagging wife get from her reluctant husband? Consider: How much do we stand to gain from nagging our son or daughter? My father used to say, "You always attract more flies with honey than with vinegar."

A far better technique than nagging comes to life in Thornton Wilder's play, *Our Town*. George Gibbs is almost seventeen and talking about becoming a farmer. His father uses a casual conversation to make a strong point and instill a lesson but without nagging. Dr. Gibbs says,

Well, George, while I was in my office today I heard a funny sound . . . and what do you think it was? It was your mother chopping wood. There you see your mother—getting up early; cooking meals all day long; washing and ironing;—and still she has to go out in the back yard and chop wood. I suppose she just got tired of asking you. She just gave up and decided it was easier to do it herself. And you eat her meals, and put on the clothes she keeps nice for you, and you run off and play baseball,—like she's some hired girl we keep around the house but that we don't like very much. Well, I knew all I had to do was call your attention to it. Here's a handkerchief, son.

A child's disobedience calls for his father's love, first, to clarify what sin is and then to understand why the son has chosen wrong instead of right. Let's assume that a father has told his son not to become a smoker. Sometime later, he finds evidence that his son isn't obeying him in this matter. Where's the sin? Not in smoking cigarettes; in and of itself, smoking isn't one of the sins God specifies, although we now know that smoking harms the body, the dwelling-place of the Holy Spirit. No, smoking is only the means of sinning—the means of dishonoring a father's wishes, the means of violating a father's trust, the means of lying about one's actions, and so on. Just as an automobile is a neutral object, so is a cigarette. But a stolen automobile is still neutral; it's the driver who is the thief, the sinner. A cigarette sneaked in an alley in contempt for a father's express command makes the smoker disobedient and sinful. So, in disciplining his son and correcting his ways, a father must deal with the real issue—not the smoking but the deception; not the cigarettes but the breaking of a promise. If the real sin is identified and rooted out, the means to sin may also be removed.

Once the sin itself has been clarified, it's also important to discuss why the child chose to break his word, to deceive his father; why did he do what he knew was wrong instead of right? Sometimes the reason he gives may be mere curiosity. Since it appears to the boy that everybody else is doing it, he wants to try it too. Of course, that's not the real reason, as we discover later; but I know a father who answered his son's explanation by saying, "I agree, you should know what it's like to smoke." Whereupon the father produced a carton of cigarettes bought for the purpose and forced his son to smoke one after another for two hours. Gagging and coughing, the boy finally emerged from the experience resolved not to take up the habit. Another father whose child-rearing methods I respect adopted a similar approach when he learned of his thirteen-year-old son's appetite for beer. "Okay, let's drink together, just you and me. I'll buy a couple of six-packs," he told his son, "and you and I can sit right here in the family room and chug 'em down. Or maybe we'll invite Mom to join us and see how much she can hold." Suddenly, all the glamor of a beer blast was gone. The son perceived that what interested him wasn't the refreshing taste or the fewer calories or the gusto life, as advertised. What he wanted was his own crowd of good friends; he wanted to be one of the boys. Yet he also claimed to believe in and belong to Jesus Christ. His father didn't need to preach a sermon; the boy could see for himself the fallacy in his own reasoning. In this instance a potentially ugly scene turned into a lesson that lasts.

Unfortunately, in every father's experience comes a time when

his son needs more than a quiet word of counsel to mend his
ways. He needs a sharp rebuke accompanied by a lingering reminder that what his father says goes! Sometimes that reminder
takes the form of physical punishment, especially at an age when
it's too much to expect a young child to follow a line of reasonable explanation. As that child grows older, both explanation and
moderate spanking may be necessary. Eventually, other forms of
punishment—the loss of privileges, confinement to a restricted
play area, even removal from one environment to another—take
the place of spanking altogether. What matters is not so much
the type of punishment as its degree. To be effective for its purpose—to correct and deter—punishment must be fair, reasonable,
appropriate to the offense, and not unduly harsh.

This doesn't mean that a father can't or shouldn't show his
emotions when he's administering punishment. Of course he
must. If there's no reason for anger, why then is the boy being
punished? Anger is one way of letting a child know that we care
about his behavior. Right behavior brings joy; wrong behavior
brings anger. There's probably nothing quite so frightening to a
child as the prospect of being beaten in cold blood by an imper-
sonal adult, someone who shows no sign of being emotionally involved. Such a person must be a sadist. A child wants to know
that the blows he feels hurt you as much as they hurt him! So we
do well to be angry and to express our anger, while at the same
time keeping in mind what St. Paul writes. He quotes from
Psalm 4:4, and says,

"In your anger do not sin." Do not let the sun go down while
you are still angry, and do not give the devil a foothold
(Ephesians 4:26–27).

That's good advice for every father—and mother too.

For punishment to be fair and reasonable, it must restore
order where chaos abounds, without causing further disorder,
without endangering the child or anyone else, and without losing
sight of the issue at hand. This means punishment that relates
somehow to the offense. If your son is habitually neat about his

clothing and his bedroom, you don't punish him for lying by making him clean the basement. You don't tarnish his virtues by connecting them with his vices. Instead you withhold his dearest privilege for a specified and limited time, making sure that he knows the relationship between his valued privilege and the paramount importance of truth.

I remember taking my sons to a nearby shopping mall, when they were in their early teens, to buy each of them a pair of shoes. Now, perhaps in their minds, this was my paternal duty, not really meriting an expression of thanks. Let me assure you, I didn't see it that way! Lory and I had brought up our children to say "please" and "thank you" with sincerity and on all occasions. So on the drive home I waited for the magic words from either boy. When it became clear that they'd both had a lapse of manners, I pulled the car over to the side of the road and reached into my briefcase for two pages of notebook paper. Handing each a sheet of paper, I growled, "Take a memo," and dictated these lines from Shakespeare's *King Lear:*

> How sharper than a serpent's tooth it is
> To have a thankless child.

Both boys were stunned; then as a light bulb went on over their heads, they began to stammer their apologies. "Sorry," I said relentlessly, "by supper tonight, I want a composition from each of you on that quotation and how it applies to taking your parents and their money for granted. And by the way," I added, "each of you owes me the full amount of the shoes we just bought. You can pay me on the installment plan." Thereafter, whenever someone was kind enough to remark on our sons' courtesy, Lory and I were amused to recall that it hadn't been developed by chance. The behavior we required came to pass because certain demands were made and reinforced when necessary by punishment.

So far as I can remember, I only once resorted to using the Bible as part of punishing my sons. Don was about ten years old, Kevin eight, and they'd been fighting over something; one of them had said something threatening to the other. I sent each to his room with orders to read Genesis 4, the story of Cain and Abel. After about a half-hour, I called them and we had a verse-by-verse exposition of the passage. By rote recitation they memorized Cain's sarcastic denial of his brotherly responsibility, and then we paraphrased "Am I my brother's keeper?" into terms that eight- and ten-year-olds can understand. They've been best of friends ever since. But, ordinarily, it's unwise to turn the Bible into a weapon of punishment or an instrument of torture with required memorization of so-many verses for this crime and so-many more for that, as some parents and Christian schools recommend.

Admittedly, our children's failings are never easy for us to accept. The reason is obvious: We measure our own success as parents by what we see in their behavior, so that when they fail, we too have failed. We hurt not only for them but also—maybe mostly—for ourselves. We take it as a personal defeat, a stain upon the family honor. We need to deliver our children from the burden of our vanity. When their actions bring shame, that shame must be their own, or else it means nothing to them. One can't repent for someone else's wrongdoing, and so when parents are disappointed by a child's behavior, that disappointment must be translated into terms the child himself can understand. Otherwise, the pain is all the parents', not the child's. When a child sins, we must restrain ourselves from overdramatizing our disappointment, so that disappointing us becomes more serious than offending God.

If our teaching and example have been based on what's found in God's Word, then we've set a standard that remains constant. Our children will know the mark from which they've fallen short. But if our standard has been something as shallow as family pride—"Don't do anything to disgrace this family!"—we're on less solid ground. Disgrace, you see, isn't a fixed commodity; it doesn't automatically follow certain preconditions. If, for instance, a son comes home with the news that his girl friend is pregnant, his parents may well feel surging tides of rage, embarrassment, disappointment, and disgrace. These are all natural emotional reactions related to family pride. But where's the expressed concern about those things that really matter: the nature of their son's relationship with the girl? her welfare and the eventual welfare of the unborn child? These are the issues of substance, and the real disgrace would be to ignore them in preference to salving one's own emotional distress. The real disgrace might come from insisting upon a marriage to legitimatize an already unhappy union, just to preserve the parents' pride.

It's easy for parents—fathers as much as mothers—who feel close to their children to wish so much for their well-being, we almost suffocate them with love. Because the line dividing our passions is so thin, even our love can become twisted into expressions almost as intense as hatred when our sons and daughters fail to live up to our expectations of them. The poet T. S. Eliot prays for us all in his poem *Ash-Wednesday:*

> Teach us to care and not to care
> Teach us to sit still . . .
> Our peace in His will.

This peace will be ours when, as father-and-son, as parents-and-children, we come to know the blessed joy of forgiveness. For punishment must never carry with it the slightest suggestion that, after proper repentance, forgiveness and reconciliation are impossible. Not in a Christian family. The Good News is that Jesus Christ forgives sins! So, with that assurance, St. Paul can write to forgiven Christians, "Be kind and compassionate to one another, forgiving each other, just as in Christ God forgave you" (Ephesians 4:32).

Some fathers are afraid to punish their sons for fear that these boys will hate them afterward. But by withholding punishment, they leave their sons in a kind of no-man's-land of unsettled conflict, unresolved guilt. Incident after incident builds into a wall separating father from son, and still the father avoids the kind of confrontation that is needed with its punishment and forgiveness that make a new beginning possible. Sometimes we don't give our children sufficient credit as reasonable human beings. They themselves know how necessary it is to rid themselves of guilt. When we've eaten spoiled food or gulped down a glass of sour milk, we can't feel comfortable until we've purged the digestive tract and our taste buds of rankness. When someone mistakenly or deliberately swallows a lethal substance, we force the poison out of his system by giving him some foultasting antidote to induce vomiting. Cathartics and emetics may be unpleasant in themselves, but they're necessary to our wellbeing. So with punishment. If a child knows he has done wrong, he isn't happy living with frustration and resentment. He wants to have things put right. More often than not, when faced by his disobedience, a son will admit his fault and accept the consequences. He knows what to expect and bears no grudge for what's fairly dished out as punishment. He needs to be cleansed of the after-effects of his wrongdoing; he wants to know the healing power of forgiveness.

But a son also knows when he's being punished unfairly, and unless he has been bludgeoned into sullenness, he will let his father know with characteristic and striking honesty. Before such a reprimand becomes necessary, we do well to pay attention to one of the most sane words of warning in all of Scripture: "Fathers, do not embitter your children, or they will become discouraged" (Colossians 3:21); likewise, to the Ephesians Paul wrote, "Fathers, do not exasperate your children; instead, bring them up in the training and instruction of the Lord" (Ephesians 6:4).

That phrase again! It seems as though we can't get away from "the training and instruction of the Lord." But looking at it carefully once more, we begin to see that Paul's concern for the way Christian fathers rear their children fits into a larger context of family life and the whole Christian community. Here the principle for governing Christian behavior begins by finding and maintaining the point of balance. Christian behavior isn't at all a onesided proposition; the scales of right living, according to the

Bible's own teaching, are in perfect balance. Look closely at what
Paul writes to the Colossians:

> Wives, submit to your husbands, as is fitting in the Lord. Hus-
> bands, love your wives and do not be harsh with them. Chil-
> dren, obey your parents in everything, for this pleases the
> Lord. Fathers, do not embitter your children, or they will be-
> come discouraged. Slaves, obey your earthly masters in every-
> thing; . . . Masters, provide your slaves with what is right and
> fair, because you know that you also have a Master in heaven
> (Colossians 3:18–22, 4:1).

When we see these statements in their full context, we discover that Paul has been urging his readers to demonstrate their
unity in Christ (Colossians 3:1–17). As an evidence of that unity,
he calls for an even flow of love or *agapē*, the highest Christian
virtue, between individuals and classes. But love is only an abstraction until it takes on concreteness in our deeds; so our love
for each other must show itself by the way we act toward each
other. Wives and husbands, children and parents (with an em-
phasis upon fathers), slaves and masters—each acting toward the
other in such a way that God's love marks the relationship. It's
not the case of someone's saying, "I'll obey you *if* you love me"
or "I won't embitter you *if* you obey me." No, it's a wife and
husband saying to each other, "I love you, and because I love
you, I can live out the expression of that love by my willing
submission, by my total dedication, to your welfare." The child
says to his father, "I love you, and I offer my obedience to you,
knowing that you have only my welfare at heart." His father
replies, "I love you, and I require your obedience so that the
Lord will be pleased with both of us; but my discipline will only
be for your encouragement and growth."

But there's another key to understanding this passage and its
application to our homes and families. Masters are reminded
that they too are slaves of a Heavenly Master. In a parallel way,
fathers must remember that they are the sons of a Heavenly Father, whom they must obey in all things; husbands are part of

the Church, the Bride of Christ, for whom the Heavenly Bridegroom gave his life.

How different our Christian homes would be if, day by day, we lived out this perfect equilibrium!

CHAPTER 7

... and Gladly Teach

No matter how ideal his father seems, every boy needs some other masculine figure to admire; every father needs another man's particular assets to help him complete the composite model of what it means to be a man. Wherever these additional characteristics may be found, no father should feel ashamed or unworthy, inadequate or negligent, because his son finds something admirable in some other man. Obviously, no single human being possesses to the maximum degree all the highest virtues of physical, mental, emotional, or spiritual power. In each of us some weakness exists alongside our strengths. In one man, his weakness might be an insensitivity to the arts or a lack of interest in sports; in another man, an obsession with work to the exclusion of recreation. Someone else may display a coolness toward the church, a nonchalance concerning achievement in school, an inability to express affection, a scornful attitude toward so-called "woman's work" such as cooking or gardening. In my case, it's a woeful clumsiness with tools that spells one of my weaknesses.

Whatever the problem, one of the secrets of success at being a father is knowing your own liabilities and discovering somebody else's strength; then letting the expert teach your son what you can never teach him. For some boys, that expert may be found within the family itself—a grandfather, an uncle, an older brother. In other instances, the search for a fuller representation of manhood may include, by necessity, men outside the immediate or extended family—a Scouting leader or camp counselor, a neighbor, pastor, or teacher. In our family, we've relied on many such men. College students working as summer camp counselors and woodsmen at Deerfoot Lodge in the Adirondacks; the neighbor next door who sees a potentially dangerous situation and cares enough about somebody else's children and their well-being to make it his business; a university campus rector named Peter James Lee, who notices a young man's spiritual interests and gets him involved in teaching a Sunday School class; a theatre director, Neil Akins, who never lets a young actor settle for less than his best. These are some of the men who've been teachers to my sons.

Let's go back to that matter of tools. I'm a fumbler without peer when it comes to anything mechanical. As Al Mead said, I don't know which end of the hammer to hold. For me, replacing a light bulb is a major feat of engineering; you should see me trying to change a typewriter ribbon. When our children were young, they often suffered without the toys their playmates enjoyed, not because we couldn't afford to buy them but because I couldn't face the humiliation of not being able to fit Tab A into Slot B. If I hadn't located a bicycle shop that actually took pity on people like me and would put the bikes together, our kids would never have owned them either. As far back as grades seven and nine, I'd earned distinction as the only boy in either class—at two different schools—to fail the shop course. My excuse, naturally, was my father. He was no better than I at hammering a nail. "How-to-do-it" books weren't part of his theological library. Having learned nothing from him about changing washers or repairing a switch, it's no wonder that my tool kit today consists of a screwdriver and a pair of pliers, kept in the same drawer as the telephone book.

My sons would have been condemned to perpetuating our family's mechanical awkwardness to at least the third generation, if it hadn't been for the circumstances of where we live. Our home is on a boarding school campus, where three dozen families live closely as a community. Among my colleagues are some men blessed with both mental and manual dexterity; they know how to use tools well. One man refinishes old furniture, another turns driftwood into lamps; two or three can tune an automobile engine, and so on. Our drama director can not only build a set from scratch but also assemble and hang a bank of lights wired to a control panel he has designed. All my work comes from the head. Certainly, writing is tedious, even laborious, but in a physical sense, until a book is published, I have little to show as the work of my hands, the result of my physical labor. Simply by observing these other men at their avocations and sometimes becoming involved with them in their professional duties, Don and Kevin have learned that some teachers do other things besides sitting at a typewriter hour after hour. Fortunate the father whose son finds in a teacher those qualities that augment his own; but all teachers aren't to be found in schoolrooms.

From their earliest years, living in our family's apartment in a boys' dormitory, our sons also admired the men on our school's maintenance staff. One of their favorite Christmas presents, when they were three and four years old, was a toy tool belt with plastic hammer, wrench, and all. For weeks they went around wearing this badge of the skilled mechanic and fighting between themselves for the honor of playing the role of our plant superintendent, "the fixer man," as they called him. Between college terms, the only summer job either of them wanted was to join the maintenance crew, working under Bob Traina with Sergio Penzi and Gus Wolff.

Together and individually, these men have taught my sons that they don't have to go through life as awkward as their father. Under their watchful guidance, Gus and Serge's apprentices have reconstructed a whole corridor of rooms in a dormitory, installed artificial ceilings in classrooms, tiled a roof, constructed a chemistry lab with all its plumbing and electrical work—plus all the common digging and hauling and other grunt-work of an ordinary laborer. My sons now have certain manual skills and experience their father never dreamed of, skills whose value, in purely practical terms, is inestimable. But what greater lessons they've learned!

Because Sergio Penzi and his partner Gus Wolff take pride in their work, they also take pride in teaching a beginner the right way to accomplish a task, with efficiency and a minimum of wasted time and materials. Yet in every job that Kevin and Don have done with their foremen, the boys have been granted the luxury of making a few mistakes while they learn, realizing that the price of an error in this kind of work can be far more costly than a spelling mistake on an English test! Because of Gus and Serge, my sons have also learned to appreciate the comradery of work, the depth of care for each other's welfare on and off the job, the mutual concern for another man's family, the quickness of reflex and presence of mind that must always accompany a man at work with his tools. Most of all, they've learned to respect the dignity of skilled labor and the integrity of earning honest wages from the sweat of a man's brow. For these and other moral lessons, I hail Sergio Penzi and Gus Wolff as masterteachers, among the great ones my sons have been privileged to know; more than this, I thank them for being surrogate fathers, filling in the gaps where I could not contribute to my children's upbringing, teaching them lessons they could never learn from me, while never undermining a son's respect for his father.

Why are teachers so indelibly etched in our memories—the bad ones along with the good, the merely competent with the masters? Why are so many pages in biographies and personal narratives devoted to rehearsing the stories of schooldays with recollections of "reading and writing and 'rithmetic, taught to the tune of a hickory stick"? Isn't it because our teachers hold such power over us as children, they sometimes exceed even the power we acknowledge in our parents? Isn't it because, in fact, our teachers seem to claim an almost divine authority over us? Alfred Kazin, recalling his childhood in Brooklyn, writes in this vein:

All teachers were to be respected like gods, and God Himself was the greatest of all school superintendents. Long after I had ceased to believe that our teachers could see with the back of their heads, it was still understood, by me, that they knew everything. They were the delegates of all visible and invisible power on earth.

Wielding such leverage, whether consciously or not, teachers can scarcely avoid imprinting their attitudes, their opinions, their style, upon children.

A child's thinking and character are pliable throughout the years of formal schooling. As Alexander Pope wrote,

> 'Tis education forms the common mind:
> Just as the twig is bent, the tree's inclined.

That's why a totalitarian government insists upon uniform schooling for indoctrinating its citizens. The state shields its children from influences it considers corrupting. For instance, in preparation for the 1980 Olympic Games in Moscow, the Soviet Union announced that all school children to the age of twelve would be evacuated from Moscow's environs so as to protect them from distraction and foreign influence.

To us in a free society, this seems absurd. We allow a multiplicity of voices to call out our children's names and claim their attention. But while many influences are beneficial, we too would agree that some are deleterious to our children's welfare. If we could, we might very well choose to shield our children altogether from the worst of these. In the past, the voices most listened to were the child's own parents; then his teacher's and pastor's voices; then those from the culture around him. Today, without question, the dominant influence upon children is no longer the home, the school, or the church; today, it's television, with too many crass appeals to everything common and cheap, vulgar and vain. Next comes the peer group, with its ethics and fashions determined by popular music and films; thereafter, and at an ever-increasing distance, come the school, the home, and perhaps the church.

Enough has been written and said decrying the crippling effect of television addiction upon our youth to make it foolish of me to add another word. But allow me just two paragraphs, if you will. Everything wrong with America has been blamed on television, from the decline in scores on the College Board tests to juvenile violence and Satan worship. We all know what we could do: Blind the Sony Trinitron 23-inch Cyclops by pulling the plug and canceling our subscription to *TV Guide*. But that's the extreme remedy, comparable to amputating an arm because of a hangnail. That's the same approach to the problems of living in this world advocated by all who would seek "the achievement of a Christian life, apart from civilization," as H. Richard Niebuhr writes in *Christ and Culture*. For some Christians, as Niebuhr shows, from Tertullian at the beginning of the third century A.D., to the monastics, and on to certain branches of the Mennonites, this has been the prescribed course of action.

I suggest that such a radical solution is a father's easy way out for the time being. In the long run, it won't solve the problem of whether or not your child is going to grow up knowing how to make a wise decision concerning the value of his time, the value of his mind, the eternal worth of his soul. No, I don't advocate keeping a cobra in the corner of my family room—as some extremists like to charge—just to teach my children to be wary of snakes. But neither do I dupe myself into thinking that I've taught them to avoid the triviality and outright dangers of television programming by forbidding them to watch it. For the truth is always this: What is forbidden in my home becomes all the more attractive in somebody else's house. Instead of forbidding any television viewing, a father should monitor and control some viewing, keeping his authority to turn off the set as he deems best. But at the same time he should be giving his children some responsibility for being selective in their viewing, making their choices in conformity to what they are learning about the Bible's standards for morality.

Back to schooling and the influence of teachers: I've already written a couple of books on that subject; I don't propose to write the same again here. Just let it be said that it's up to us as parents to keep alert. You should know who educates your child and how well he or she is doing it. Because the law compels us to give our children some form of schooling, we most often thrust them into the care and keeping of total strangers, adults about whom we know nothing more than their names. Some authority—the local board of education and the school principal —has validated a university transcript and other credentials, then hired these people to teach our children. More often than not, a teacher turns out to be reasonably competent, and for this we can be grateful; at least, he or she doesn't prevent our child from learning. Once in a while, a misfit shows up in education, a person who has no business dealing with other human beings in a learning situation. When this happens, the results can be dismaying to both students and parents. If not corrected, the effects of one bad teacher may thwart a child's desire to learn.

But occasionally—if you are blessed—your child will meet a teacher whose effect upon your son is like spontaneous combustion. The result will be a young mind's flaming forth with incandescent energy, sparked by intellectual curiosity, igniting his imagination. You'll see in your son's face and hear in his voice an unmitigated pleasure at sharing with you a new idea he has learned from this teacher. When this occurs, give thanks!

Your child's encounter with this special teacher can happen very gradually, sometimes without the child's even realizing that he's being drawn toward a new dimension in his education, the experience of learning with joy! Contrary to television's stereotype of the effective teacher, he may not be as charismatic as a Joe Namath or as witty as a Gabriel Kaplan or as comical as a Bill Cosby or as idealistic as a Ken Howard. In fact, when you meet your son's favorite teacher, you might be quite surprised to discover how ordinary he seems—not terribly "with it," not necessarily "cool," maybe even a trifle "different." When you ask your son, "What's so special about Mr. Smith?" he may not be able to give you a very revealing reply. "I don't know," he may stammer, "I just like him." The proof of that remark, however, will be evident in the obvious concern your son begins to give to his work for Mr. Smith's class. You may hear him saying things like, "I didn't used to like science, but with Mr. Smith, it's okay." You won't need to wonder why.

The late Archbishop Fulton J. Sheen, himself a teacher nonpareil, spoke of the importance of lucidity in teaching—making a lesson clear and plain. But lucidity isn't enough to cause a person to change his attitude toward learning, his attitude toward life; for that to happen, said Fulton Sheen, "the self of the teacher has to make contact with the self of the hearer." This doesn't mean that, in order to motivate his pupils to learning, a teacher must become their pal, any more than a father can be effective by misrepresenting himself as his son's playmate. What it means is that the truly effective teacher is the one whose character penetrates through the lessons he teaches, so that he and his subject are one. For every real teacher's subject isn't what he knows but *who he is.* Integrity in teaching means giving a student the whole package: not just the externals of pedagogy and scholarship but the character of the teacher as well.

Someone has said that the mediocre teacher tells, the good teacher explains, the superior teacher demonstrates; but the great teacher inspires. My first great teacher—the first man other than my father—who inspired me was Donald Davidson. In some respects, I owe him my life.

At twelve, I was a wispy eighth grader living in Toronto, Ontario, struggling to overcome both the common neuroses of any early adolescent and the seemingly special problems that made me unhappy. For during that period following World War II, my father was seldom at home. He had given up being a pastor and had become a traveling representative—"deputation secretary," in our religious jargon—for a mission agency working with lepers. His territory spanned all of Canada and half the United States; sometimes he was on the road for as much as two months at a time. A single deputation tour in 1950, for instance, might sweep through Eastern Canada to Halifax, down to New England and the Middle Atlantic states, out to the Midwest and back to Ontario by way of Winnipeg.

Throughout my early- and mid-teens, I was essentially without a father's presence most of the time. Dad became someone to whom I wrote letters; in return, he brought me felt pennants for my collection, souvenirs from his distant ports-of-call. True, we traveled with him in the summer, but apart from these trips and other rare occasions when his meetings might be within driving distance of where we lived, my mother and sister and I were seldom with him. In memory, I see my father boarding a Canadian National train, his bursting Gladstone bag in one hand balanced by a Bell and Howell 16-mm projector in the other—and always a black homburg riding at a careful angle above his lean face and reddish mustache. He never seemed quite as saddened as I by his departures.

We had moved to Toronto from Haslett, Michigan, where Dad had been the pastor of the only church in our village. With my mother as town librarian and my father judging like Samuel in Shiloh, everyone knew the minister's family. It was a secure situation, and I'd revelled in being the preacher's kid. Those years, from 1943 to 1946, are still crystalline in my memory because, I suppose, it was a time when even young boys were thinking about life and death in real terms. The gold star in a neighbor's window meant that Sergeant Jerry Truax wasn't coming home; but Captain Cleo Buxton, fighting with General Mark Clark in Italy, was still safe. In that Michigan town I joined the Cub Scouts and cheered Dallas Canfield and Lindy Cousins, our Haslett High School basketball stars, in the state tournament; I memorized two hundred Bible verses to earn a free week at summer camp and won a war bond for selling the most subscriptions to the old *Pathfinder* magazine; I even walked off with a chocolate cake at the 4-H Club's winter fair.

This was also the time when I first became aware of girls and couldn't decide between Janice Miller and Patty Piper, so that by the time I asked first one girl, then the other, to go with me to the sixth-grade picnic, they'd both accepted invitations from other boys; I got stuck with a fat girl whose name my mind has blotted out—or did she get stuck with me? I recall the epidemic of ringworm in our area. One day, my class was taken to a darkened room in the school basement to have our scalps examined under an ultra-violet lamp. One by one we were led to the eerie center of that room to have our hair pulled back and a verdict given. I can still hear the shriek of dismay when Wendy Cousins, the most beautiful girl in sixth grade, was told that she would have to have her long blonde hair cut off and wear a skull cap.

I remember that Mrs. Martin, my sixth-grade teacher, brought a radio to class so that we could listen to the final game of the 1945 World Series. In the first inning, when the Detroit Tigers' catcher Paul Richards hit a double that cleaned the bases, we cheered our heroes' triumph over the Chicago Cubs. But what I remember best is the momentous day in August, when the war with Japan finally ended. To celebrate, I organized the ringing of our church bell. Hour after hour it pealed. I pulled the rope until my hands were raw. Then our family jumped into the 1939 Oldsmobile and drove into Lansing to join the spontaneous frenzy of joy at the state capitol.

Life in Haslett, Michigan, could not have been more happy. Then, suddenly, it was all over. Moving from that tiny town to metropolitan Toronto—leaving behind my sixth-grade classmates in mid-year—devastated me. I was a Canadian by birth, but I rejected the idea of returning to "our home and native land." In fact, whenever my new school was called together in assemblies to sing "O Canada," I showed my spite and chauvinism by mumbling the words and melody to "Michigan, My Michigan." Because of the postwar housing shortage, we had no place of our own to live, and so, for reasons unknown to me, our family boarded for several months with a widow and her adult daughters. My sister and I shared a room, and we were kept informed by our landlady that we occupied somebody else's house. No amount of rent could buy the privacy for which we yearned. As part of a series of crises, including the collapse of my schoolwork, I became an almost chronic bed-wetter, thereby compounding my shame and anxiety.

At last, reprieve from the widow's boarding house and her everlasting diet of pigs-in-blankets! The mission found us first one

house, then another more suitable, in the East York section of
Toronto. Somehow I managed to be promoted from sixth to seventh grade, then on to eighth. As the beginning of the term
approached, that fall of 1947, I prepared myself to endure the
ordeal of starting all over again—another house, another school,
another set of classmates, another adjustment, but always the
same frustrations, the same loneliness. This time, however, the
experience would be different, for my new teacher would be a
man who doubled as principal of Chester Public School. My
mother walked with my sister and me to the school that first day
and took us both to the principal's office, where I met Mr. Davidson. He was tall with a white streak through his graying hair.
His voice reverberated off the walls of his office. "I'm sure we'll
find a desk for you, Bruce, and you'll do very well here at
Chester." He smiled, and with that smile my world lighted up.
Something about this man—his deep-set eyes, his hearty laugh,
an indescribable warmth of genuine affection for his students—
communicated itself to me instantly. If ever a young boy needed
to be welcomed and encouraged, that boy stood there before
Donald Davidson, and the man did not fail him.

Mr. Davidson taught our class only part time; his secretary
took over while he did his administrative work. I can't remember
a single classroom lesson, except I know that he stressed the importance of our knowing history and seeing the rush of current
events in the light of that knowledge. From him I learned about
Jacques Cartier and Samuel de Champlain and the rest of the
French *voyageurs,* and of Wolfe the dauntless hero who had
defeated Montcalm on the Plains of Abraham. At this news we
English-speaking Canadians whooped it up and vowed to keep
any francophile Quebeckers in their place.

Midway through that year, Mr. Davidson conducted a public
speaking contest in our class, with both prepared and impromptu
speeches required. Unknown to us, our winner would represent
the school in a city-wide oratorical competition. With my
mother's help, I put together a talk about last summer's trip to
the United States Public Health Hospital at Carville, Louisiana—

the American leprosarium. Certainly my subject was unique. Mr. Davidson declared me the local winner and set out to prepare me for bigger things. He worked on my delivery and to help overcome my stage-fright, he took me to larger schools to practice in their empty auditoriums. When the city-wide contest was over, and I'd gained only an honorable mention, I felt that I'd disappointed him and wasted his time. But he smiled that warm smile, patted me on the shoulder, and said, "All Chester School is proud of you!"

But what I remember best about Donald Davidson was the way that he merged being a teacher and administrator with being an athletic coach. I'd never seen that combination before; in fact, I had an idea that sports and studies were somehow inimical to each other. But here was my teacher and principal, with all his other duties, coaching our softball teams—three squads divided by weight classes. At 87 pounds, I qualified for the lightweight team, but as the best catcher in the school, I also played on the two heavier teams. Most of my expertise in softball had been gained at summer camps and Bible conferences, where I'd also learned a line of chatter to encourage my pitcher and interfere with the batter's concentration. My sportsmanship, however, ran somewhat behind my volubility, and I found myself in frequent disputes with umpires. At one of Chester's games, the official umpire failed to show, and so the two coaches took turns umpiring. Mr. Davidson stood behind me, and soon my stream of nonsense got on his nerves. After I'd complained a bit too earnestly about the quality of his vision, he stopped the game and called me aside. "Lockerbie," he growled, "I should tell you that you and your team are losing the benefit of the doubt on every close call because of your mouth." I shut up.

Late in the spring, word came that Toronto's grade schools would hold a track meet. Mr. Davidson informed my best friend, Stuart Eccles, and me that we would compete in the hundred-yard dash for boys twelve and under, as Chester's only two representatives. Neither of us knew anything about the sport of track and field, although I had always done fairly well at Sunday

School picnic races. But I'd never been in a real track meet on a real track. Mr. Davidson decided that we needed coaching in the fundamentals of sprinting—starting fast, running in our lanes, and finishing with a lean at the tape. Following a softball game, he asked us to meet him back at the schoolyard after our evening meal. By the time Stu and I arrived, our narrow strip of playground, overhanging the steep Don River valley, had been transformed into a sprint straightaway. Somewhere Mr. Davidson had obtained a lime roller and marked out two lanes the length of our field. Each evening that week he worked with us. On the day of the meet, held at the University of Toronto's Varsity Stadium—ah, dreams of Olympia!—our teacher and coach said to us, "Remember, boys, start fast, run courageously, and finish strong through the line!" In my first—and last—formal competition as a sprinter, I managed to place second in my event. Only seven years later, I returned to that same track to win the Canadian national eight-hundred-meter championship, and as I rounded the final turn at the open end of the stadium, I could still hear Donald Davidson's challenge, "Run courageously."

The last time I ever saw him was only a few weeks into my ninth grade at nearby East York Collegiate Institute, our neighborhood high school. Mr. Davidson had learned from my sister's teacher that our family was moving once again, this time to London, Ontario. He sent a message through Jeannie, asking me to come to his office for a chat some day after school. I went, not knowing that my former teacher had asked for a set of grades from my current school. The marks weren't good. As had become my custom, whenever faced by an impending household move and change of school, my interest had slackened. I'd known for some time that I wouldn't be at East York much longer; my work had become negligible. Mr. Davidson looked up over his bifocals as I entered his office. He dispensed with all niceties and got right to the point. "Lockerbie, I have before me a surprising report of your grades at East York. I want you to know that Chester School expects more of our English prize-winner than shows here! Can we count on you?" I gulped back a lump of tearful embarrassment and assured him that I would try harder. Then he softened and said, "I want you to know that, wherever you go, you are one of my Chester boys. Never forget that fact!"

There was no formal farewell. He hadn't called me to his office for sentimental reasons. What he had to say applied wherever I went. Nobody had ever expressed that kind of lasting interest in me before; no one other than my parents had ever challenged me to keep a high standard for its own sake. He was the first to make me care, to make me want to do my very best. Donald Davidson, my first mentor. He was there when I needed him.

The teacher your son or daughter most admires is almost sure to be a person who gives more of himself or herself than the union contract calls for. Young people today are looking for leadership from people who believe in something, who are willing to put their lives on the line by giving time to what they claim is important. Your child wants a teacher who takes his teaching seriously, who is well prepared for classes, and treats his homework assignments, tests, and term papers like precious documents. Your son doesn't want to see the work he's labored over given a cursory reading and a check-mark. He'd rather have his paper crisscrossed with notations and marginal inquiries; he wants to know that he made his teacher sweat a little in the give-and-take of education. The most successful teachers I know don't read the daily paper while their students are writing a composition in class; they write the essay along with their students. Why shouldn't they, if writing is as important as they claim? Such evidence of academic commitment, however, can no longer be taken for granted, and so when your son finds a teacher willing to offer a bit more encouragement, your son has found a friend. The same is true for teachers who sponsor the stamp club, coach a soccer team, take extra time to prepare a clarinet soloist or actor or debater; or teachers who simply show an interest in their students by being present at a school concert or football game, when they don't have to be there. That's what really proves to a boy that his teacher cares.

The hallmark of every great teacher is his personal quality of kindness. It was this quality, perhaps more than any other, that drew me, first, to Donald Davidson; then, two years later, to the man whose humane and dedicated teaching God eventually used as a model for my own vocation.

A few days following my last conversation with Mr. Davidson, our family moved from Toronto to London, Ontario, where I enrolled at Central High School. As usual for me, the fall term was already well under way. To help me adjust to my new surroundings, the counselor—a friendly little man unforgettably named Merton Entwistle—inquired about my interests. In those days, my goal in life was to become a radio broadcaster, perhaps a missionary working with Clarence Jones at the great pioneer station HCJB, the "Voice of the Andes," in Quito, Ecuador. Through my father I'd met Clarence Jones at various missionary conferences; I'd been fascinated by his trombone playing as much as by his evangelism, "Heralding Christ Jesus' Blessings" by means of shortwave transmission throughout the world. But if not missionary broadcasting, then my alternative ambition was to become a sportscaster like Bill Stern or Harry Wismer or Foster Hewitt, the play-by-play announcer for each week's "Hockey Night in Canada," featuring the Toronto Maple Leafs: "He shoots! He scores!" With this information, Mr. Entwistle encouraged me to join the school's Studio Club, a group of budding broadcasters and technicians who were responsible for setting up microphones for school assemblies and intercom announcements from the inner sanctum, the office of the dreaded Archibald MacKillop, principal of the school.

Our club also provided qualified operators for 16-mm movie projectors, a skill I already possessed from countless times of showing my father's films of leprosy victims and his mission's work among them. One of the Studio Club's standing engagements was to appear with a projector and screen at the girls' health education classroom. There the projectionist would be handed a film never catalogued in our files and told by the woman instructor to thread the film into the projector, start it rolling, and then leave until invited to return and remove the machinery. At first I was puzzled, until a classmate and fellow club member, Ted Flint, informed me that this movie and others like it introduced the girls to the mysteries of menstruation or other wonders of the female anatomy. Knowing absolutely nothing about such matters myself—except for the few titillations I'd received from missionary films of bare-breasted pagans—I was curious to become informed also. Ted taught me the trick: By deliberately fouling up the threading of the film, one could force the teacher to call the operator back into the room, where he would have to remain at least long enough to catch a glimpse of the next few scenes. Thus Studio Club made it possible for me to obtain some part of my sex education one frame at a time.

The sponsor of our club was David Carr, the most popular teacher in the school. We called him "the Duke," although never to his face. He looked like an aristocrat, an independent man of the world. He was a bachelor in his late forties, we guessed; tall and gray-haired with a close-clipped gray mustache that made him seem to us very much like a magazine model for Hathaway shirts, except that he wore no eye patch. He'd been an officer in the Canadian Army, much decorated according to student say-so, although he never indulged in telling us any of his wartime heroics. "The Duke" was also a musician, a pianist who could cover the repertoire from a Chopin etude to current show tunes; in fact, if memory hasn't entirely slipped, I believe that it was David Carr who first showed me the structure of bass progressions in a "beat-me-Daddy-eight-to-the-bar" boogie-woogie. I know he used to accompany the school choir and also played for school-wide assemblies, at which we'd all sing by reading the lyrics flashed on a screen. At these occasions we'd finish by standing to sing Central's fight song, written by Mr. Carr:

> There's a school in our fair city
> Whose fame is spread both far and near,
> And though other schools win favor,
> There is none to us that is so dear . . .

When we reached the last note of the chorus, we'd catapult ourselves back into our seats and in a ritual of loyalty guaranteed to engender school spirit, bend over and shout into the floor—for greater resonance, I suppose—an incantation to transfix our opponents by its magic spell:

> Purple and Gold, Purple and Gold,
> Hit 'em in the wishbone, knock 'em cold!

Sitting at the piano onstage, David Carr was not too stuffy to join us in our cheer, another indication to us that he was a real man.

I didn't get to know the Duke well that first year, but I was overjoyed to learn, at the beginning of tenth grade, that I'd been selected for Mr. Carr's honors English class. Ever since my eighth grade experience with Donald Davidson, I'd begun to appreciate being taught by men. I had no particular aversion to female teachers, just a preference. As a matter of fact, I'd never been taught by a male English instructor. All my previous English teachers had been unmarried women, some quite enjoyable as schoolma'ms go. But from them I'd somehow acquired a set of misconceptions about literature and composition. Their poems were full of "hidden meanings" and other enigmas to be unlocked only by knowing the difference between spondaic and dactylic—or was it iambic?—and other such technical matters. The act of writing, I was told, called for a certain aura of solemnity largely achieved by the use of big words and awkward syntax. Furthermore, writing itself was secondary to such larger concerns as parsing sentences and drawing diagrams of them.

The Duke was different. His teaching left no room for sighing over the classics; he was too busy making sure that we were being caught up in the adventure of reading, bringing words to life and staging our own productions of *Treasure Island* and *The Charge of the Light Brigade* in the theatre of our imagination. In his classroom, during tenth grade and half of eleventh grade—until, once again, my family moved on—I learned to appreciate the power of a word; from him, learned the remarkable effect that reading aloud can have upon an audience, especially when that reading receives dramatic intensity, as was always true in his class. So, from his teaching, Sydney Carton and Charles Dar-

nay strove as rivals for the love of Lucie Manette; the ro-
guishness of Sir Toby Belch and the poignant absurdity of Sir
Andrew Aguecheek were more real than my Sunday School
teacher's droning piety. At David Carr's insistence I committed
to memory innumerable lines of poetry, some of which I've never
forgotten, some of which I've drummed into the ears of my own
offspring and other young men; such as this stanza by A. E.
Housman:

> Up, lad: thews that lie and cumber
> Sunlit pallets never thrive;
> Morns abed and daylight slumber
> Were not meant for man alive.

Or these obscure lines by Austin Dobson:

> Farewell, Renown! Too fleeting flower,
> That grows a year to last an hour . . .

We learned *The Highwayman* and *The Death of the Hired
Man* and Tennyson's *Ulysses*:

> . . . Come, my friends.
> 'Tis not too late to seek a newer world.
> Push off, and sitting well in order smite
> The sounding furrows, for my purpose holds
> To sail beyond the sunset, and the baths
> Of all the western stars, until I die.

How could he or I have known that the last poem he assigned
for us to memorize, a sonnet by Richard Le Gallienne, would
prove to be so prophetic? It was *Brooklyn Bridge at Dawn*:

> Who, seeing thus the bridge a-slumber there,
> Would dream such softness, like a picture hung,
> Is wrought of human thunder, iron and blood?

Before memorizing these lines, I'd crossed the Brooklyn Bridge
during two or three visits to New York City. But I didn't know—
nor could my teacher—that at that very time, my father was

weighing an invitation to become pastor of the Bay Ridge Baptist Church in Brooklyn.

The Duke also taught us to write better than we had written before. He never slighted the conventions of English grammar; but while we learned that nouns might be the names of persons, places, or things, we also became aware of something none of my previous teachers appeared to have understood: that all the knowledge of grammar piled book upon book has never yet produced a single well-written sentence. To learn to write, one must write. So David Carr made us write. When the city newspaper, *The London Free Press*, put out feelers for "stringers," sports correspondents to cover each of the four local schools, Mr. Carr recommended me as Central's reporter. My first by-lines came during the basketball season of 1950–51, with my teacher and backer hailing every published word.

In Studio Club, in English classes, I came to know David Carr well; but we had other opportunities to become acquainted beyond the confines of the classroom. He had a cabin in the woods a few miles out of the city; I remember that the boys in Studio Club hiked out there for a weekend with the Duke. He took us to football games at the University of Western Ontario, and there were English class picnics at Springbank Park. He'd traveled widely and taken better than amateur films of his journeys. They were silent movies, of course, but he was a master at narrating his travelogues. He hired me to be his projectionist at various library, church, or other community lectures and always paid me generously.

But I suppose I got to know him best by working around his house on Saturday mornings, weeding or doing other garden chores, or stripping wax from his hardwood floors. His housekeeper would prepare a hot meal—how well I recall her potato pancakes!—and the morning always ended with the three of us sitting at the Duke's kitchen table. At one of these Saturday noon meals, Mr. Carr inquired about my parents and home; I don't know what prompted him to do so, other than genuine interest. His question and the kindness which he had already shown me caused me to well up with emotion; to my great embarrassment at that time, I found myself spilling over with tears in an outpouring of my unhappiness. For if my father found exhilaration in his work and its constant travel, for us at home his vocation was taking its toll. Prolonged absence—six weeks, eight weeks at a time—repeated over and over during the children's maturing years strains any family's fibre. My sister and I were both growing up in a family in which our parents scarcely saw each other more than a few days every two months. In a more secure home, perhaps, such separation might have made less difference; in our home, however, we never knew when the moving van might be arriving. Our father's absences did not inspire confidence or encourage us to make lasting friendships.

My mother has always been a resourceful woman. Living with my father, she had to be! His restlessness, his transient "pick-up-and-go" attitudes, his resistance to any hint of permanence made it impossible for her to acquire much sense of contentment. "This World Is Not My Home, I'm Just A-Passing Through" was one of E. A. Lockerbie's favorite songs. Meanwhile his wife did the packing.

Furthermore, my mother bore more than her share of the family's burdens. She was expected not only to care for the home and children but also to maintain the bookkeeping and correspondence from my father's work; then too, she was commissioned to accept as many local speaking engagements on behalf of the leprosy mission as possible. These pressures, compounded by loneliness and frustration, drove my mother to stomach ulcers and a bitter spirit. In these latter years, she has learned the grace of sharing her experience with others who have been blessed by her many books and personal warmth, but Jeanette Lockerbie herself will admit that the mid-1940s and early 1950s were not happy years for her or her children. Adding to her emotional distress was our constant financial uncertainty. In spite of the large sums being transmitted monthly to mission headquarters, my father's stipend arrived with less and less regularity. Fortunately, our house was large enough to allow an upstairs apartment to be rented out; students from the London Bible Institute, two blocks away, occupied another couple of rooms. This income paid the mortgage. Most of my earnings from work for Mr. Carr and other odd jobs went to help with the food budget.

But just that week, I'd splurged with some of my money and bought a flashy bow-tie with which I hoped to attract Betty June Campbell or Donna Blackwell into sitting with me at a Saturday night youth meeting. The tie never had a chance to work its charms, for when my mother saw it, she assailed my selfishness and shallow sense of values. Didn't I know how poor we were? That very morning, on my way to work for Mr. Carr, the tie had been returned to the haberdashery; its cost would be reclaimed for the family coffers.

For years, at missionary conferences, I'd heard all about "living by faith" as members of a "faith mission." Now our family was experiencing the day-to-day reality of what those phrases mean. To be sure, when contrasted with the poverty and privation others endured and are enduring, our circumstances were luxurious. We were taught to pray for patience, relying upon the God who fed Elijah, who stayed the widow's oil and flour; we knew the fulfilling of the Psalmist's claim, "I was young and now I am old, yet I have never seen the righteous forsaken or their children begging bread" (Psalm 37:25). So what if I couldn't afford the bow-tie or the football cleats I yearned for, and so was laughed at for being the only player in the huddle wearing sneakers? But it would have been so much easier to endure if only my father had been there to share my humiliation.

I told David Carr much more than I'd intended. When I began to regain control of myself, I noticed that the housekeeper had left us alone. Mr. Carr looked directly at me and said, "It will all work out, but you must be strong for your mother's sake." He didn't extend my chagrin with any more advice, but, nodding toward the door, dismissed me. As I rose to leave his table, he handed me my usual payment, a Canadian two-dollar bill, or so I thought. Not until running to the bus stop did I look and see that it was ten dollars. I knew that it was no mistake, but when I ran back to thank him, the Duke simply said, "Don't waste it on any more bow-ties!"

I never saw David Carr after February 1951, when my family left Canada. We moved to New York City. I became an American citizen by naturalization, married an American girl, and ended my Canadian boyhood. But I've never lost my profound sense of gratitude to the Duke for all he taught me—not just its content but also its manner. For this man, this father-figure, taught with energy and enthusiasm, with imagination and integrity, but most of all, with kindness. If I could be one-half the teacher he was, in the full dimension of all he meant to me, I would consider myself to have emulated him well; for David Carr remains my model of what a teacher should be: a friend.

Your son may find such a friend among his teachers in almost any school, for throughout the public schools of this nation there are still dedicated teachers—persons for whom the welfare of their students is more important than peripheral issues such as union agitation and school politics. Admittedly, such teachers will be a distinct minority in these days when so much of our society seems preoccupied with looking out for Number One. Surely, however, Christian teachers in the public schools can be counted on to be a schoolboy's friend, someone "who sticks closer than a brother" (Proverbs 18:24). You and your son will know who these teachers are; they'll stand out from others in their profession by their integrity, their refusal to be clock-watchers, their sense of Christian vocation as salt and light in a corrupt and darkened world. While he teaches, the Christian teacher will also continue learning. These are two sides of the same coin, inseparable conditions for every real teacher of whom, like Chaucer's Oxford clerk, it may be said, "And gladly would he learn and gladly teach."

There's no getting away from it: The best teachers are those who have never lost their own love for learning. They bring to whatever they do much more than sheer enthusiasm, because enthusiasm is only a vapor that can be blown away by the winds of discouragement; more than energy and imagination, because these too can falter and grow weary. The best teachers are fueled by nothing less than love, which shows itself by their desire to share with everyone else what they already know and are still learning about the world. "While we teach, we learn," said the Roman philosopher Seneca. By this very cycle of teaching-and-learning-and-teaching, educators can be kept from growing stale, bored by the same old stuff year after year; for while Euclidean geometry or the text of *Moby Dick* may remain the same, and while the causes of the American Revolution may be unchanging, two other factors in education are always variable: the relationship between the teacher and his knowledge, and the relationship between the teacher and his class. In the best schools—the sort of school that is right for your child—teachers believe that their subjects are important enough to be taught and learned; they're devoted to enlarging what they know about their disciplines. But such teachers care even more deeply about the students they meet every day—not just as students but as persons with whom they are learning as they teach.

But perhaps by nature, such a spirit of selfless giving in teachers may be found more frequently in schools which claim to be Christian. Not only so, but such so-called "Christian schools" should also be representing a different standard of excellence and a different philosophy of education by which to instruct your child. As a result, Christian teachers in these schools are free to be direct in their witness, open about relating their behavior to faith in Jesus Christ. A Christian school's standard—and therefore the standard by which its teachers live—should be nothing short of what the Bible assesses as "whatever is true, whatever is noble, whatever is right, whatever is pure, whatever is lovely, whatever is admirable"; in short, as St. Paul writes, "if anything is excellent or praiseworthy—think about such things" (Philippians 4:8).

One of the towering figures in education was Thomas Arnold; his work at Rugby School, in the early nineteenth century, reformed the English school system. Arnold said, "The great work of education is to make us love what is good, and therefore not only know it but do it."

What often motivates your son to love his teacher and wish to emulate his or her knowledge is the tremendous power of example. In his famous address, "The American Scholar," Ralph Waldo Emerson said, "Only so much do I know, as I have lived. Instantly we know whose words are loaded with life, and whose are not." The genuine teacher is someone interested in learning, not for learning's sake, but as part of life's unending search for truth—learning as *right action*. Because this teacher lives out his art or her science—not merely teaching music but making music, not just teaching history but being a historian—that teacher's own life confirms that what he knows is *good*, or else he wouldn't spend his time doing it! A boy's admiration for this person's example causes him to equate the whole quest for further knowledge with what is good and honest and worthwhile in life. A teacher teaches his pupil to "love what is good" by showing, not telling. Discrimination is the ability to make wise choices, and the greatest influence any teacher can provide is the example of knowing what is good, then doing it.

Every adult—not only those who call themselves teachers—has this same responsibility. But to help point the way to truth, the guide himself must know in which direction to search. For to know what is good and to do it, one must first come to know God, who is the source of all goodness. In his treatise "Of Education," John Milton, author of *Paradise Lost*, summarized the philosophy of Christian schooling in these words: "The end, then, of learning is to repair the ruins of our first parents by regaining to know God aright." But to do this calls upon a Christian teacher to be more than a Big Brother or a United Way volunteer. A Christian teacher must show his love for Jesus Christ by loving the children he teaches—yours and mine—and by being an example of Christ-like living to them.

Christian teachers in a Christian school will realize this obligation. Without preaching in their classrooms or otherwise distorting their academic responsibilities, they'll nonetheless point toward order where moral chaos would reign; they'll call for submission to God's sovereignty in place of man's disobedience and anarchy; they'll attempt to redeem another generation from perpetuating Adam's rebellion by pointing to the Cross and the Empty Tomb. To do all this, they'll need our prayers and support.

CHAPTER 8

Run . . . to Get the Prize

In his poem *The Bee*, James Dickey describes a father and son walking along the shoulder of a California highway, dangerously close to the traffic careening by. Suddenly the young boy cries out in pain. A bee has come out of nowhere and stung him. In blind frenzy he darts out into the oncoming stream of trucks and cars, hoping to shake off the bee-sting. Instantly his father sprints after his son, spurred on by an echo in his mind recalling his old football coaches' screams at a scrimmage against the varsity. James Dickey's poem is dedicated "To the football coaches of Clemson College, 1942," and, he tells us, relates a true incident. In that moment he realizes how much coaches are like fathers: "They want you better/Than you are."

I may be prejudiced on several scores, but I favor James Dickey's comparison between coaches and fathers. First, as an athlete—schoolboy, collegian, and adult—I've benefited from the fatherly concern of several coaches. Next, as a coach myself, it's been possible for me to help some of my runners who've needed paternal guidance as well as athletic training. Certainly, my experience as a father of athletes bears out the analogy. Our sons and daughter have participated in football, wrestling, basketball, swimming, and field hockey, as well as track; in college, each of them has been a member of the University of North Carolina track team. Growing up on the campus of what was at first a boys' school, their earliest understanding of what older boys do was gained at school sporting events. When they became old enough to ask for particular baby-sitters among the students, they almost always chose their favorite athletes. With their play-mates—other faculty children—they had ready access to every kind of sports equipment and facility near at hand. They went to summer camps where sports were a large part of the program. Not surprisingly over the years, as these children have matured, Stony Brook's teams have learned to rely on a nucleus of faculty sons and daughters to be leaders. In my twenty-five years at Stony Brook, I can't recall a single faculty member's son who hasn't been a varsity athlete; the participation among daughters is almost as high.

But these observations aren't limited to polling my own kids and their friends. Everywhere you look, the young people who seem to be enjoying the happiest, most wholesome teenage years are those whose schooling has room for sports, or perhaps music, theatre, or student government, as well as their studies. Not to the exclusion of everything else, but in proper perspective the experience of organized team play and individual dedication to physical training can make an enormous contribution to develop-ing character.

For all we hear and read about today's careless youth, with their presumably indifferent attitudes, the fact is that partici-pation in interscholastic sports is at an all-time high. Organized community sports—basketball, baseball, football, and soccer teams, AAU swim clubs, as well as Junior Olympic track and field teams—are also booming. While intercollegiate athletics may appear to be for the elite minority of superstars, even there a serious-minded candidate is welcome to try out for a team. Be-yond college, our golf courses and bowling alleys, our public ten-nis courts and swimming pools, not to mention our roads and running tracks, are crowded with adults seeking either exercise or competition. Only a dozen years ago or so, a middle-aged runner along the roadside would have been a spectacle subject to catcalls from passing motorists; today, the sight of more than ten thousand men and women in a six-mile road race or a twenty-six-mile marathon is no longer unusual. Economists and marketing experts forecast that sporting goods will continue to be a growth industry for the remaining years of this century.

Why such interest in sports? What makes so many young people in particular give themselves to the taxing physical training and mental stress of competition? Surely not the delusion of wealth from stardom as a professional! So few players, for instance, make it to the National Basketball Association's less than two dozen teams, how could any playground hot-shot justify his hours of practice for that goal? Is it the possibility of seeing one's name in the newspapers, even the local weekly? That's more reasonable. So is the pleasure of walking through the school corridors wearing a varsity letter-sweater or jacket. But these are all superficial reasons. Talk to young athletes themselves, and more often than not they'll speak of more significant factors that motivate them to train and compete.

"I like feeling healthy and fit," says Cindy Graham, a high school all-star in field hockey and volleyball. "Some of my friends are content to loll around the house or just hang out somewhere together or maybe ride around in cars. But I enjoy the feeling of getting my heart really pumping and my skin tingling. It lets me know that I'm alive, that my body is real. I get that from being in sports."

Another reason for participating in sports is the lasting comradeship it builds. "I like the people in sports," says Dennis Fulton, whose game is soccer. "They're my best friends. I know a few other guys in school who aren't out for any team, and they're okay. But my friends, the people I really know, are the guys on my own team and the other guys you meet in the locker room. You get to appreciate them because you know what they're going through—the same as you. You know they're putting out their energies and their time every afternoon to improve themselves and the team. Sure, some of these athletes are jerks and some of them fool around with dope, but most of us in sports have stayed away from that stuff.

"Something else," Dennis goes on, "in sports you get to meet people from other schools, even from other countries. While the game is on, you're out there trying to knock them off their pins, trying to block their shots right back in their faces, really playing tough. But after the final horn sounds, we've got something to share, something to talk about, you know?"

Every athlete of whatever age knows this common bond among sportsmen. Some of the men I respect most are men against whom I struggled hardest in races a quarter century ago. Every once in a while one of them turns up on the starting line of a master's race today—for in my mid-forties, I'm still tying on my shoes for the New York Athletic Club. When I see someone I remember well from a generation ago, it gives me joy to know that both of us are still well enough to be able to compete; then comes the old competitive urge, the will to run him into the ground! After the race we may discuss our families and our work like old friends, but for the moment we're competitors once again. For me, it's rejuvenating.

But for many young people one of the principal reasons for their participating in sports is a person, the coach of their team. Often this coach's influence is as great as their parents', sometimes even greater. Why? Because a coach and his athletes meet at a point of genuine importance to these young people. If athletes know that their coach really cares about his team and their overall welfare, they'll listen to him, even when he's talking about other matters: homework, grades, behavior, appearance, getting on with parents, and most of all, spiritual concerns.

A coach can show how sports may be an aid to academic study by teaching an athlete, first, that learning to play hockey or run the hurdles begins by mastering the fundamentals. You can't become a leading scorer without first learning how to handle the hockey stick, how to pass and control the puck, how to shoot with power and follow-through. You can't win a hurdles race without learning how to clear the first barrier and then maintain your balance and speed for the next hurdle. The same is true in algebra or biology or chemistry, in English or French or German. You learn one step at a time, starting with the first step.

A coach teaches the value of commitment. There's no such

thing as a half-hearted athlete; either he gives a sport his full effort during practice and competition, or else he's wasting everybody's time. Furthermore, coaches of contact sports tell me, the football player who holds back just a little during tackling drills or scrimmages is much more likely to be hurt than the player who goes all out on every play.

A coach expects his athletes to be present at every practice on time and ready to participate. An athlete learns this responsibility; he understands that he can't just show up whenever he feels in the mood. As a result, an athlete usually makes wiser use of his time for homework than does the non-participant, just because the athlete knows he doesn't have all afternoon and evening to get it done. He knows that he'll be tired after practice and will have to be in bed an hour or so earlier than others; so he looks for study time during a free period at school or in place of watching a currently popular TV show.

I asked a boy in my English class the other day what sport he was going to play this season. "I'm taking the season off," Wally told me. "My father wants me to improve my grades, and he won't let me go out for any team until I have a higher average." Too bad, I thought. Whenever I hear of parents making this demand, I question its wisdom. A young boy like Wally needs physical exercise and seldom gets enough in physical education class as an alternative to competitive sports. But just as important is the waste of psychic energy and loss of morale a boy suffers when he's forced to discontinue playing. Furthermore, it equates academic study with punishment. It's a father's delusion to say to his son, "This season, instead of putting on the pads every afternoon, you're coming straight home from school to hit the books." It just won't happen; or if there's a semblance of effort—an open textbook and a boy leaning over it—the amount of real learning going on will be less than might be supposed. Why? The boy's heart isn't in it. He's thinking of his classmates and would-be teammates on the football field or wrestling mat and wishing he were there. Yes, it's true that some few boys may buckle down and really work hard enough at their studies to earn a father's reprieve; but I'd be willing to put my neck out and say that, more often than not—at least at Stony Brook—the next report card shows little or no improvement; certainly not sufficient to have merited sacrificing the benefits of a season's play, with all the other lessons to be learned.

Being on a team teaches cooperation and dependence on others, along with the responsibility to pull your own weight. This is true even in the so-called individual sports, such as fencing or swimming or wrestling. You don't have to play doubles in tennis to know that your every serve and stroke is contributing to your team's score in the match. A teacher may struggle to convince a reluctant student to speak up in class and share what he knows on the grounds that his classmates are depending on him; a coach has no such problem in convincing his athlete.

An athlete also learns the value of perseverance, sticking it out to the end. One of the most important lessons we try to teach in coaching runners is to run *past* the finish line. The natural tendency is for the body to rejoice that its hard work is almost over and to coast on home in the final few strides. At the end of a close race, an opponent who's willing to gut it out all the way can rob a leading runner of his place, if that runner slackens off, applies the brakes, and eases down. It takes mental fortitude to keep saying to oneself, "Run right through! Don't slow down!" To help an athlete's weary mind, a coach stands by the track and hollers these words for him. But if the runner doesn't say it for himself, he can ignore the coach's warning and suffer the consequences. Sometimes disappointment is the best teacher.

Another kind of perseverance means hanging tough even when you want to quit—not just the race or match today but the whole sport. Almost every spring somebody on the track team sidles up to me and mumbles something about dropping off the squad. I always give such people the same advice: "Sure," I tell them, "why not? It's a free country. Nobody here can compel you to run or jump or throw against your will. This isn't East Germany!" I look to see the flicker of a satisfied smile in the corner of his mouth, suggesting that this quitting business is turning out to be easier than he'd feared; so then I say, "But before you quit track, make sure that you understand what you're doing. You're not just quitting a sport; you're not even quitting a team. You're quitting *on* the team, and that's a different story. You're quitting on people who are counting on you, people who've given you their time and concern, people who've identified with you as a teammate. But more than this, you're also quitting on yourself. Do you know what that means? That means it's always easier to quit again instead of seeing something through."

By this time, usually, my disheartened team member is really squirming and looking for some worm hole to crawl into; but I'm just getting revved up! "You see, the person who quits a sport just because it's tough is the same person a few years later who decides it's inconvenient to go on taking rigorous college courses or to show up for a demanding job or to maintain his responsibilities in a marriage. A quitter decides to quit just because it doesn't feel good anymore or isn't working out the way he'd hoped. Once a quitter, always a quitter."

Sounds heartless? Maybe so, but that's part of being a coach; in fact, that may be the best part—not the daily workouts or filling in a batch of entry blanks or driving a team home from a disappointing loss or even winning now and then. The real victories are those that come from teaching an athlete what St. Paul, nearing the end of his life, meant when he said, "I have fought the good fight, I have finished the race, I have kept the faith" (2 Timothy 4:7). What's more, athletes are prepared to listen when a coach talks about ultimate issues such as religion and Christian faith. From time to time, I have opportunities to address a summer camp for cross-country runners or speak at a sports banquet or to professional football players just before their game. I find that my audience isn't interested in hearing a lot of jokes or in my reminiscing about my exploits as a runner. What gets and holds their attention is a clear statement of how personal faith in Jesus Christ makes it possible to "run with perseverance the race marked out for us" (Hebrews 12:1).

A coach can say all these things and be listened to, often with greater persuasiveness than an algebra teacher or a pastor or even a father. The reason for a coach's effectiveness is *immediacy*. A sports season lasts only a few weeks, three months at most. What's to be done in order to have a rewarding season has to be done *now!* So it all comes down to discipline and its practical results. It won't do any good to start getting serious just before the final game. An athlete has to get serious the moment he signs on the team. Choir and band conductors or play directors can use this same argument: If we're going to give a performance on November 15, we'd better get cracking on learning our parts. But algebra teachers and the rest of us don't have the advantage of facing quite this same kind of deadline; so it's easier for a coach to teach the rewards of discipline. This is why some athletes may respect in their coach what they reject in their fathers, especially if our sons can't recognize any immediate goal we might have in mind. So, as fathers, we ought to capitalize on a coach's teaching method, looking for step-by-step improvement toward a specific goal.

There should be a carry-over between sports and other areas of life. Listen: a real athlete—a person with the kind of inner discipline and determination to get up every morning and do fifty push-ups or run three miles before breakfast—this person can certainly be expected to pick up his socks and make his bed without being nagged. No matter how many trophies he collects, he's no champion if he can't conquer his own sloppiness. He knows this, of course; his coach has already told him, and so you can back it up with your own high expectations.

At its best, what your son sees in his coach is a dimension of the father-son relationship we all need: mutual encouragement. It's easy, of course, to encourage a winner, to exult in what "Wide World of Sports" calls "the thrill of victory." But what about "the agony of defeat"? What happens when Johnny strikes out with the bases loaded in the bottom of the last inning? How do we react when Billy misses the free throw that might tie the basketball game? What's our frame of mind when Tommy forgets his lines in the school play or when Steve's tuba booms forth at just the wrong time? That's when a father's character is really on the line. His son finds out whether Dad loves him or just the prizes he sometimes wins.

In March 1980, I had occasion to test this truth at first hand. Kevin's one-mile relay team had qualified to compete in the National Collegiate Athletic Association indoor track championships, and I went to Detroit to see him run the lead-off leg. Before Kevin's event, a runner from Baylor University, unable to control his speed on the banked turn, nose-dived off the track and hit a row of bleachers. Unconscious, he was carried to a hospital, where he received fifty stitches to close the gash in his leg. It was a sobering reminder that any sport has its dangers. Sitting there in the new Joe Louis Arena, I prayed that my son would be spared such a fall, that he would run his best. As the gun went off, Kevin blazed around the first turn faster than I've ever seen him fly. Suddenly, as if he'd stepped on a cherry bomb, he shot straight up, gripping his left thigh. A muscle strain had knocked him and his University of North Carolina team out of the race.

I sat staring at him, paralyzed by my own disappointment, knowing his grief. But in that very moment, an old competitor from high school days, Joe Toles of Auburn University, was there to help Kevin. His teammates also gathered quickly to lift him toward the training room, where a doctor treated him; opposing coaches stopped by to wish Kevin a full recovery.

It was some time before I saw my son in that training room under the huge arena. Many thoughts had coursed through my mind. "Why, God? What purpose does it serve? How does a boy's injury glorify you?" But when I saw Kevin, I realized how much stronger he was than I. While his leg hurt, his greater pain was for his teammates and for the unknown runner from Baylor. In his personal anguish, he was experiencing a cleansing unselfishness that helped to purge the bitterness of my frustration. "I don't understand what the Lord's trying to teach me, Dad," Kevin told me later that night. "Maybe I'll know in a week. But

I'm sure glad you were here to share it with me." Whatever help I may have been to him, his strength encouraged me.

Of course, not every boy is an athlete or wants to be; nor should he be made to feel inadequate if he's not an all-star candidate for the pros! Some fathers, usually retired jocks themselves, push their kids into sports of their choosing and pressure them to practice skills for which the youngster's muscle systems aren't ready. I know a father who dressed his three-year-old in a Dallas Cowboys football uniform, complete with helmet, shoulder pads, jersey, and padded pants. The toddler could hardly move with all that gear on. Much to his father's disgust, the child was afraid of the football being thrown at him. Frankly, it was a little hard to tell one three-year-old from the other!

We all know instances of parents' becoming too involved, especially in sports. At a wrestling tournament, our school's heavyweight competitor was facing one of the best wrestlers in the state. His mother, a large, red-haired woman, was very much in evidence throughout the meet, but when her son stepped onto the mat, she went wild. Her voice, like a klaxon, penetrated through all other cheering as she urged him to break his victim in half. Suddenly Stony Brook's wrestler, a much smaller boy by comparison, made a move that landed the favorite on his back. In a flash that mother was out of the stands and on the mat, beating on her son's opponent and screaming. Her husband, opposing coaches, the referee, and finally her son all were needed to steer her out of the gymnasium.

Another example. When Kevin was about ten, he and his friends Will, Phil, and Mark all entered a race sponsored by the county Department of Parks. Both girls and boys the same age were competing. The race was to take them around a college soccer field and into a wooded area, then back, about a mile in all. As we arrived, I noticed one father and son who seemed terribly serious about the event. The father especially behaved as if he were coaching a prospective Olympian. He hovered over his son's every move in warming up for the race; at the starting line, the boy could hardly pay attention to the starter's instructions because his father kept yelling out signals of his own. The race went off, and as it turned out, this boy wasn't really in a class with his competitors, one of whom was a very fine runner indeed, a girl. As the children came out of the woods and raced toward the finish line, this father's calls of encouragement changed to ugly threats: "I'm warning you!" At the finish the boy was still panting when his father rushed over, grabbed him, shook him, and then slapped him twice across the face. "Don't you ever lose to a girl again!" he screamed.

That kind of intensity is manic, a perverse form of paternal sickness showing itself in child abuse. But you don't have to be neurotic to encourage your son in sports. Given a natural environment and a freedom from the pressure to win at all cost, most boys will find pleasure in kicking and throwing a ball, in jumping and running. Their leisure play will soon involve their own organized games and the choosing of sides. When they discover that certain skills are required to play these games as well as other boys, that's the time to show them how; not forcing it on them but as the need arises. Eventually their physical education teachers will help to develop their coordination and refine their skills. When the school begins to establish teams and competition coached by its own teachers, a boy should be encouraged to try out for the team, if he has any affinity for sports at all—just as the same boy should be encouraged to try out for a part in the school play or choir. We never forced participation in sports or other activities on any of our children; we let them know, however, that we expected them to be active and productive in their use of time—no sitting around the house watching television every afternoon.

If your son makes his school team, all well and good. Let him know that you'll do your best to attend his games and cheer for his team. But if he doesn't make it, that's no disgrace. He can try again, or he can devote his energies to something else just as important. In my case, I tried again, but not until I'd been given some coaching at home—from my mother! For it was she and not

primarily my father who created in me enough pride and desire
to want to succeed in my sport.

I'm getting a little ahead of myself, but I can best illustrate my
mother's dedication to helping me by telling you this story. In
the fall of 1955, I was captain of New York University's cross-
country team, a team strong enough to contend for the National
Collegiate Athletic Association title. The NCAA meet was to be
held at Michigan State University in East Lansing, near my old
home in Haslett. NYU's athletic director, Jim Gilloon, wasn't sure
that the budget could afford to send a full cross-country team of
seven runners such a distance for a weekend. Only five runners
actually score, so NYU agreed to pay the train fare for five if
we'd put up the expenses for our hotel and meals. My mother,
never daunted, wrote to her sister-in-law, Evelyn Lockerbie, in
Lansing, asking her to take us in, to which Aunt Ev agreed with
typically warm hospitality.

As captain, I was entrusted with the train tickets. I arranged
to meet my teammates at Grand Central Station, where we'd
take the overnight express to Detroit and from there continue on
to East Lansing. But driving from our home in Brooklyn to Manhattan, my father became snarled in a traffic jam on the West
Side Highway. By the time he'd wriggled free and began heading across town, it was only a few minutes to "All aboard!" Still
several blocks away from Grand Central, all seemed lost, but I
decided to make a run for it. As I bolted from the car, I realized
that my suitcase and running gear were in the trunk. For a moment I hesitated, knowing that I'd never be able to cover the distance in time carrying luggage. My father shouted from the car
window, "Never mind, we'll take care of it." I arrived at the station platform just as my teammates were preparing to hang me
in effigy. We sprinted through the closing gate and made it to
our Pullman car.

Next morning, as we walked through the Detroit depot heading toward our Grand Trunk connecting train, my mother hailed
us. When I'd left them, my parents had driven to LaGuardia Airport, and my mother had taken a plane to Detroit. Where they'd

found the money, I have no idea. In her hand she held my suit-case with my track equipment. I owe her the third-place NCAA medal I took home that weekend.

It all began in that nearby Michigan village, under the apple trees surrounding our Baptist parsonage. I'd come home from school—fifth grade, it must have been—with the news that I'd been chosen last for the recess softball game. The reason? Not that I was the new boy in town, a foreigner from Canada; not even that I was the preacher's kid; just because I couldn't catch the ball. I was afraid of it.

Afraid of a ball? That was all my mother needed to hear. Thereafter, every evening following supper, she took me outside to where the ground was strewn with wormy apples fallen from the trees and made me play catch with her. The rules were stern: We stood only a few feet apart until I'd caught ten throws without dropping one; then we both moved farther apart and began another set of ten. If I dropped one apple, we took a step closer and started all over again. The eventual object, not at-tained for several weeks, was to be able to stand fully 60 feet apart, the distance of our softball bases from each other. Some-times an apple she chose was half rotten and would smash as I caught it. But if I so much as flinched, I lost another step. It wasn't quite the same as learning to play at one of today's high-powered sports camps, but I learned to catch nonetheless. From that time on, I lived almost solely for sports.

In 1945, I also became aware of professional sports, hockey and baseball in particular, with loyalties divided according to my alien status. As a Canadian I maintained my affection for the Toronto Maple Leafs, but as a Michigan resident I cheered the Detroit Tigers. Both teams accommodated me by winning their respective championships, the Stanley Cup and the World Series. I saw neither team play in person. For all my father's in-terest in sports, we seldom attended any games other than our high school's schedule, which we never missed.

My only connection with these teams, therefore, was through the broadcasts of their games; yet so attached was I to the players, so familiar with them, one might have supposed that Syl Apps and Turk Broda were my uncles, that "Prince Hal" Newhouser and "Doc" Cramer were my older brothers. I kept scrapbooks of clippings and photographs for each team and became something of an encyclopedia of sports information. Sometimes I knew more than the radio announcers describing the game, and I wondered how they could be so stupid. From listening faithfully to each game, it was an easy step to living out my loneliness and social inferiority by fantasizing an athletic prowess I didn't possess.

Football became my first love. High school, college, or professional—American stars like Otto Graham and Marion Motley across Lake Erie in Cleveland, or Canadian heroes like Joe Krol and Royal Copeland of the Toronto Argonauts—it didn't matter who was playing. I was right there on the field with them. Often by half-time, I'd have become so worked up by the announcer's account of the action that I'd leave the radio and go out into the street or nearby park to reenact the game's highlights—and miss the entire second half. Once, however, I made it to the "Super Bowl," Canada's version called the Grey Cup game, in person. One of my father's missionary friends, John Russell of the Sudan United Mission, knew my fanatical love for the Argonauts and understood my need for a substitute in my father's absence. He somehow obtained tickets to the championship game, pitting Toronto against the Winnipeg Blue Bombers. (Want to know the score? Toronto 10, Winnipeg 9, won by Joe Krol's kick late in the game.) Years later, perhaps John Russell found the thrill he gave me repaid as he cheered my winning anchor leg in a championship race at the Penn Relays in Philadelphia.

But attending the Grey Cup only stirred my ambition even more to rise above being a spectator; I hoped to be a football star myself. I envied the strength of Dale Creighton, the speed and balance of John Sweeney, London Central's football demigods; but frankly, my illusions far exceeded any reasonable measurement of ability. The spirit was willing, but, at 103 pounds, the flesh left a good deal to be desired. Still, I faithfully took my scrawny body with its limited assets to practice every afternoon and actually made the squad as a reserve defensive back. The truth is, I was the last name on the roster to receive a uniform. Wisely, my coaches hardly ever chose to inflict my cunning and strength upon the opposition. I did have one moment of glory, however, intercepting a pass in Central's stomping of arch-rival London South, and running it back for a few yards before disappearing under an avalanche of enemy jerseys.

Thereafter, for the most part, my exploits were contained within my own imagination, although I also lived on the fringes of athletic success as my school's sports correspondent. My bedroom became the first all-weather stadium. There, using a quilt marked out in geometric patches, I sponsored and competed in various imaginary sports events, facing the greatest athletes. All the time these fanciful games were going on, I kept up an appropriate commentary as the play-by-play announcer.

So my heroics passed unnoticed, locked in the privacy of my mind. When I returned briefly to London, a half-dozen years later, having won the Canadian eight-hundred-meter championship in record time, a newspaper interviewer tried to discover an angle, something like "local boy makes good." But it fell flat. In doing his background research, the reporter discovered that my former coaches could scarcely recall that I was even on their teams. They had every right to forget; nothing they'd ever seen suggested that Bruce Lockerbie might be an athlete. I don't blame them now for failing to have seen any potential. Instead, I regard it as part of the remarkable providence of God, for the fact is that I probably would never have become a real athlete at all, if my father hadn't decided to leave Canada for Brooklyn.

On February 28, 1951, our family crossed the Canadian border at Fort Erie, Ontario, to Buffalo, New York. For the second time, we officially became alien residents of the United States of America. That day my life took on a new direction. If I'm grateful to my father for nothing else, it's for leading his family to the Bay Ridge Baptist Church. There he introduced me to a girl whom I loved at first sight, who stood with me at its altar and became my wife, the mother of our three children. At first, however, I'd been full of resentment over making another move, suffering another uprooting. I was just beginning to feel at home in London, just beginning to develop a teenager's independence. I'd miss my friends; I'd miss the activities at church and school; I'd miss the Duke, my teacher David Carr. Furthermore, for all my protestations over missing my father, I'd begun to question my own sincerity. Having grown accustomed to his absence, I had no great desire to live under his constant scrutiny. The last thing I wanted was to be the preacher's kid again! Inwardly I raged against my father; outwardly I sulked. As the time for our move approached, I resolved to spite him where it would hurt him most, his pride. I'd read a raunchy novel called *The Amboy Dukes* and from it had obtained my vision of what Brooklyn would be like. Once we got there, I determined to rebel against my father's authority, join a marauding street gang, take up with coarse women, and break his heart.

Instead, I met Joe Kottman, the track coach at Fort Hamilton High School, close to where the Verrazano Bridge now spans the Narrows leading into New York harbor. I recognized at first a kindly man; I came to know him as a wise philosopher and builder of character rather than a molder of athletic champions. It didn't matter to him that I was a spindly weakling on whom a track jersey hung like a flour sack. If I wanted to be a runner, he would work with me. As a matter of fact, I had no idea of becoming a runner and no immediate opportunity either. New York City's high school coaches were on strike that spring, and so there were no teams, no interscholastic sports. However, our physical education classes were being closely watched by the regular coaches to see that recognized athletes received some kind of conditioning and instruction in skills just in case the strike ended. Coaches were also on the lookout for newcomers who might be invited to join the team when regular competition resumed.

In one of these classes Mr. Kottman saw me running the usual

warm-up laps with which each class began. He commended my
easy running style and urged me to sign up for the cross-country
team in the fall. I'd never heard of cross-country running before.
He also suggested that, in the meantime, I compete in an upcom-
ing Parks Department track meet to be held on our school track.
I was ending eleventh grade and hadn't run a race since the hundred yards in Toronto three years earlier. But buoyed by his encouragement, I decided to enter both the half-mile and one-mile
runs. My performances were notable only because they left me
so much room for improvement: 2:48 in the 880, 5:48 in the
mile. My career as a runner had begun. I never found the
Amboy Dukes.

When school reconvened in September, the coaches' strike had
been settled, but Mr. Kottman had decided against taking on the
cross-country team. The man in charge had probably never
coached anything before and had no idea of how to make us fit
to run two and a half miles over Van Cortlandt Park's hills. Our
work-outs, twice a week, never varied: We ran ten laps around
our quarter-mile track—the full two-and-a-half-mile racing distance—as fast as possible; on Saturdays, we'd run our races.
Needless to say, my inexperience as a runner left me without
much reserve, and I found the whole business so tedious, so disa-
greeable, that I decided to abandon running altogether; I'd play
on the church basketball team instead.

But one day in early December, just as the winter indoor track
season was getting under way, Mr. Kottman nabbed me in the
school corridor. "I'm looking forward to seeing you at practice
today," he told me and then proceeded to give careful directions
to the Naval Reserve armory where Fort Hamilton's runners held
their indoor work-outs. I'd never run indoors before; I was curious to know what it was like and flattered to have been invited
by the coach. I went that first time, never expecting to return.

"Nothing comes easy," Joe Kottman used to say, and it seemed
to apply best to the sport of track. If cross-country had been
difficult, it may have been only because the hills were steep and
the distance long. But an indoor race in a New York City armory

is as close to war as I've ever come. The gun goes off for a thousand-yard race, and a pack of twenty runners sprints for the first turn on a flat and slippery floor. Down goes one unfortunate, and three others hurdle him, hoping he'll remain prone until the game of leap-frog is over. Shoves from behind, elbows from alongside, and the flailing back-kick of the leading runners keep you wary. The air is dustfilled; your mouth and lips soon feel as if they'd been grazed by sandpaper. You lose count of laps and fall into a mindless shuffle, spun along with the pace of others who go streaming by. Then the gun fires again, signaling the final lap, and it propels a sudden burst of adrenalin through your system. Coming off the final turn, it seems as though you might have just enough sprint left to catch that boy in red and white. But he hears you coming and manages to summon an acceleration that saves himself from finishing last.

"Men are made by overcoming disappointments," Coach Kottman also used to say, but I wondered if he could be right. Then came the turning point. At the New York Athletic Club meet, to be held in Madison Square Garden, there would be a special relay race featuring five high school teams from throughout the City. Joe Kottman took our team, which boasted only one authentic runner, my friend Dennis Gatto, to the tryouts at another dingy armory. To our mutual surprise, we qualified to run among the giants at Madison Square Garden. I could hardly believe it! Madison Square Garden—the mecca of sports! For years I'd listened to the Friday night fights broadcast from the Garden, accepting every word of Don Dunphy's blow-by-blow description. Madison Square Garden was the home of the New York Rangers, the New York Knickerbockers. Now I was to be a competing athlete there too. Eat your heart out, John Sweeney!

Strange combinations of events coalesce to make a life. For me as a Christian, the fact that I trust in our God means that he's in ultimate control. But I tremble to imagine what might have been the course of my life if I hadn't taken my coach's invitation to join the high school team; or if Joe Kottman had been too lazy or indifferent to bother taking us to that qualifying tryout. I'd never

have had the experience, on February 9, 1952, of competing in
Madison Square Garden and all that followed thereafter. As I
entered the old arena, then on Eighth Avenue at Forty-ninth to
Fiftieth streets, I had a sense of the holy, for its history had become my dogma, its sports stars my gods. Here was I, a less-
than-mediocre runner stepping out of the same locker rooms that
had been graced by the presence of Joe Louis and Gordie Howe
and George Mikan; setting foot on the same track as my newest
hero, "The Flying Parson," Gil Dodds, still at that time the
world's indoor record-holder for one mile.

We finished fourth out of five teams that night, but we con-
soled ourselves with a reminder of how many other schools
hadn't even qualified. For my part, I had found my sport. I
vowed that I would return to run in the Garden. Over the next
dozen years, I was able to keep that vow; then, in the grace of
God, another dozen years later I could cheer my own sons in
Madison Square Garden.

My father soon caught my enthusiasm, but even so, he was always a lap behind my mother. Until that night at the Garden,
he'd taken a rather limited interest in my plodding around the
track. But Dad always had an eye for the Big Time, and from
then on, he seldom missed a meet. Occasional references in the
Brooklyn *Eagle* mentioned my being a Baptist preacher's son,
which did a good deal to quicken my father's passion for the
sport. Eventually my college coach, Emil von Elling, gave Dad a
special pass to sit at the Garden's trackside. Even there, however, he could never quite keep straight in his mind what my
times or events were. My mother was just the opposite. She had
never appreciated my life-and-death concern for the Maple
Leafs, and she had complained about the daily grime I brought
home from my futile football practice sessions. But years later, it
was always she who could recite not only final time and place of
finish in a given race but also my intermediate splits along the
way! She could also dish out coaching advice on racing strategies.

In my youth, Christians made almost no impact whatever on
national affairs, on the world of politics or entertainment. They

weren't exactly what you might call household names. The only two exceptions were a United States Army general named William K. Harrison, senior negotiator for the United Nations Command at the Korean truce talks, and the Reverend Gilbert L. Dodds, better known as Gil Dodds, the world's record-holding miler. Soon after I became a runner myself, Gil Dodds became my hero. I devoured Mel Larson's biography of "The Flying Parson," and wrote an English term paper about Dodds' accomplishments. I was especially impressed by his unashamed testimony for Jesus Christ, even in the face of his disappointment at not making the 1948 Olympic team because of injury. For a party given for my high school team, I rented a movie featuring Gil Dodds as both runner and coach. The film ended with Gil's clear-spoken statement of faith in Jesus Christ, and while the room was still in darkness, I found sufficient courage to say, "That's what I believe too." Then the lights came on. I'd given my first word of witness to my teammates, and Gil Dodds had made it possible.

As my senior year at Fort Hamilton High School neared its end, the question of college began to be discussed. Neither of my parents had gone to college, and we weren't terribly sophisticated about such matters as taking College Board exams and applying for admission. My father was eager to have me attend a Bible institute and train for missionary service, but I had another goal in mind. Gil Dodds, now retired from competition, was coaching cross-country and track at Wheaton College in Illinois. I decided that I would be going to Wheaton to follow in my hero's footsteps. Sometime in May I sent for a catalogue and application forms and was astonished to learn, first, the cost of a college education, then to learn that admissions had been closed for several months. Without proper guidance, I'd drifted past most college deadlines, but perhaps it was just as well since there was no money to pay even Wheaton's modest tuition. I thought of writing to Coach Dodds and appealing to him on the strength of my admiration and emulation. Surely he could get me in and maybe with some financial aid. But while I pondered how I'd write such a letter, an item in the sports pages caught my eye. A high school football star named David Burnham, from Akron, Ohio, had turned down offers of scholarships from thirty or forty major universities to attend a tiny religious institution in Wheaton, Illinois, where, reportedly, no athletic scholarships were granted. I was humiliated. If such outstanding athletes were attending Wheaton, why would Gil Dodds or anyone else care about a novice half-miler, even if my time had improved 35 seconds to 2:13? I put the idea out of my head.

But as the spring season neared its climax, Joe Kottman's patience with me began to show dramatic effects. In two consecutive races my time for the 880 dropped another ten seconds to 2:03. He took me to meets where I could face the best competitors in the New York metropolitan area. At one of these deluxe events, I placed fifth and discovered afterward that college coaches knew my name. What might this mean? I was afraid to think about it. Instead I concentrated on admiring my first significant prize in track, a bronze medal. When I showed it proudly to my coach, Joe Kottman shook my hand and said, "Always remember, Bruce, with that medal and a dime you can ride the subway." It costs considerably more than ten cents for a ride on today's New York City subway system, but my coach's point is still valid. Athletic recognition in its place is fine, but when you leave the arena or the field, you're just the same as the next person.

My last high school race would be the New York City championships, held at the stadium on Randall's Island in the East River. As we lined up for the 880, I knew that my parents and a special girl were in the stands praying for me. I couldn't pray, I was too nervous. Coming off the final turn in the middle of the pack, I suddenly experienced a surge of power that carried me into first place. The shock was more than I could bear! For fifty yards or so, I struggled to retain my unaccustomed position, then yielded just at the finish line to Vin Coiro of Erasmus Hall High School, the prerace favorite. But I had finished second in the City championships! I was still dizzy with delight when Joe

Kottman came to me accompanied by a little old man in a battered fedora, chomping on a cigar stub. "Bruce, this is Coach von Elling of New York University. He'd like to talk to you for a minute. I'll leave the two of you together." My coach went to join my parents, telling them about the conversation going on in the infield and the offer being made: a full scholarship to a great university.

As I left Randall's Island that June afternoon in 1952, one verse of Scripture I'd memorized years before kept playing through my mind: "But my God shall supply all your need according to his riches in glory by Christ Jesus" (Philippians 4:19). God knew our finances and knew I needed a scholarship; but to make that possible, I'd also needed a coach. Joe Kottman was God's provision for me.

I gladly accepted New York University's scholarship. My new coach was Emil von Elling, a legend among American coaches. At seventy years old, this man whom everyone called "Von" had been coach at NYU for forty years. In every Olympic Games since 1920, at least one of his athletes had been a participant; he himself had been a coach of the American Olympic team in 1948. His champions stood among the great names in the sport—Phil Edwards of Canada, George Spitz, T. Leslie MacMitchell, and the redoubtable Reginald Pearman, among many others. Von remembered them all, as well as those who had run in their shadow, down to the most seemingly trivial detail about their eating habits or other idiosyncrasies. Like Moses in old age, Von's eye was not dim nor his strength abated. He was still perfectly capable of instilling instant fear in any athlete whom he suspected of giving less than his best.

The first afternoon I stepped into his office at Ohio Field, Von said to me, "I understand you're a preacher's son. That means you won't run on Sundays. I had another preacher's son on the team back around 1920, name of Frank Gaebelein. He's head of a boys' school now called Stony Brook. He wouldn't run on Sundays, but he made up for it by working harder on Mondays. You do the same."

Von Elling had coached three of Gil Dodds' closest competitors during the early 1940s. Both Leslie MacMitchell and Bill Hulse had been indoor record-holders at the mile; Frank Dixon had been only an eyelash behind. But Dodds had surpassed them with his 4:05.3 record. "I suppose you're a fan of Gil Dodds," Von said to me one day. I admitted my admiration but went on to say that I was no less impressed by the exploits of MacMitchell, who was then NYU's Dean of Admissions, the man who had provided me with my scholarship. "Well, it's about time we had somebody at NYU on God's side," Von Elling growled through his cigar-clamped teeth. "When Dodds ran against us, poor MacMitchell and Hulse and Dixon always felt like they were taking on the whole Trinity!"

So began four years of maturing from boy to man, under the far-seeing eye of Emil von Elling.

Yet as graduation from NYU loomed before me, I faced the same perplexity many young men and women know. *Now that I have a college degree, what am I going to do with it?* The next chapter gives a fuller answer to that question, but here just let me tell you how God's grace brought back into my life a man whose influence had been temporarily set aside. Gil Dodds had remained an example to me, even though I hadn't gone to Wheaton College to run on his team. We'd corresponded occasionally, ever since I'd won a race—and with it, a key to the city—named for him on the Atlantic City boardwalk; we'd met at a couple of meets where NYU and Wheaton were both competing. Now God was opening the way for me to go to Wheaton after my undergraduate years to work with Gil Dodds in coaching, while teaching English to freshmen and sophomores and taking courses in Wheaton's Graduate School of Theology.

I expected to go to Wheaton in the fall of 1956 as a member of the Canadian Olympic team. For years I'd been preparing for the Olympic Games, to be held that November in Melbourne, Australia, and as my times for eight hundred meters improved, I was confident that when the boat sailed for Down Under, I'd be on it. I was still a Canadian citizen, but as an alien resident, I was particularly popular with my local draft board in Brooklyn. Each year in college I'd had a special hearing to allow a deferment; on one occasion, only the fact that NYU's athletic director was also a figure of some importance in the Selective Service System saved me from being hauled away on the spot. In the late spring of my senior year, when I'd been accepted for graduate studies at Wheaton, I was finally declared 4-D, a classification reserved for "idiots and ministerial students," as my draft board secretary informed me. Even then, however, the pressure wasn't off. To close my file, my local board needed a letter from Wheaton, which some functionary there refused to send until I'd filed my medical examination report to prove that I was healthy enough to enroll. The problem with this requirement was that part of the medical examination in those days called for an updating of vaccinations. I kept trying to stall the medical exam because I feared that a vaccination might affect my training and competition toward making the Canadian Olympic team.

At last, however, the word came. Unless I had final documents sent from Wheaton, my case would be reopened immediately, and I would be subject to report to Fort Dix in six weeks. With no other choice, I went to a doctor in Buffalo, where my father and mother had moved, and submitted to the full examination.

The date was August 21. On August 24 and 25, I would compete in Hamilton, Ontario, at the final tryouts for the Canadian team. On August 23, the smallpox vaccination began suppurating and spreading its poison through my system. I went to the starting line with fever and other elements of a classic reaction. I ran poorly, and the Olympic Games went on without me. But I grieved that the Lord had let me down. Hadn't I trusted in him with all my heart? Hadn't I committed my way unto him? Why, then, hadn't he directed my path to Melbourne? Why hadn't he brought to pass my heart's desire? My uncle John Honeyman drove me home from the stadium, empathizing with my disappointment, yet without anything spoken, flooding me with affection.

The next week I'd planned a day that was to have been a pilgrimage of joy. Gil Dodds worked each summer at a camp in the Adirondacks; I'd made arrangements months before to visit him there after the Olympic tryouts—to celebrate my success in making the Olympic team and to discuss our working together at Wheaton. Now, in the aftermath of my defeat, I longed for some way to avoid meeting a man who, eight years previously, had known the same disappointment and had conquered it. I didn't want to conquer my defeat; I preferred to wallow in it, to make myself and everyone else around me miserable in my disappointment. So I telephoned Gil Dodds to tell him that I was canceling our appointment.

But, as I was to learn, Dodds could be a most persuasive man; and so, when I got off the bus at Schroon Lake, he was there to meet me. Our greeting was like father-and-son, although he was only seventeen years older. His strong handshake and open smile won my confidence. Here was no sentimentalist offering me a crying towel. This man knew that the best way out of the Slough of Despond is to avoid falling into it, to keep on rejoicing in the goodness and grace of God and leave all the whys and wherefores to him. Gil never once asked me to recount the story of my collapsed dream. Instead he occupied our time together with talk about how my continued running might be a help to him and an inspiration to members of Wheaton's team. He spoke of the coming season with such hope that he drove out of my mind all desire to dwell upon the past. I left him at the end of that August day, having been helped over a barrier to personal maturity and spiritual growth by a man who had surmounted it himself.

We spent a year together, during which I served my apprenticeship in coaching track. He taught me the dynamics of handling a team while at the same time maintaining concern for each individual athlete's needs. Gil agreed to be my coach also, and my running thrived under his inspiration. Driven by a new sense of joy in loving God with all my strength, I was able to run with freedom and power, rejoicing as a strong man to run a race. No wonder I achieved my best performances in distances from eight hundred meters to ten thousand meters. In post-

Olympic competition that winter, against men who'd made it to Melbourne, I knew the thrill of defeating them. By the end of the indoor season, I'd posted the second fastest time in the world for a thousand yards.

But what I learned most from Gil Dodds during that year was his example of prayer for and with his team. As a Christian, Gil Dodds knew that spiritual fortitude obtained through faith in Jesus Christ was the source of his strength. He'd often astonished autograph seekers by adding to his signature such cryptic references as "Phil. 4:13," leading at least one sports fan to wonder what had been so special about a 4:13 mile in Philadelphia. As a coach, he continued to demonstrate the certainty of God's promise. He's tested it and found it to be true; what he knew he shared with others. In turn, those of us who learned from Gil Dodds have been able to pass along to young people with whom we work this assurance: "I can do all things through Christ who gives me the guts!"

Lory and I were married that same year. From Wheaton, we came to Stony Brook. Here our family has grown from infancy to maturity, blessed by a stable home in a loving Christian community. Here our children learned their Scripture verses and nursery rhymes and ABCs, their cheerleading formations and football plays and lines for *The Music Man* and *Death of a Salesman*. Here too they learned how to work hard and play hard in their studies and sports. In time, each of them knew the joy of earning a medal in the New York State track championships, and their competitive experience has carried on through college and beyond. Why did they succeed as runners? Something inherited from their old man? Some natural consequence of seeing their father as a runner and emulating him? Perhaps. But in my heart I believe the answer lies elsewhere. I think Don and Kevin, and Ellyn too, became champions because of a coach who believed in them and took them even farther than their fancies had imagined.

His name is Marvin W. Goldberg. By the time we arrived, in 1957, he'd been at Stony Brook for a dozen years, after teaching and coaching in various Long Island public schools. A chemistry teacher when we first met, Marve Goldberg was also Stony Brook's director of studies and college placement counselor, as well as coach of track and cross-country. The school was smaller in those days, only a hundred sixty students, all boys. Still he could field a cross-country squad of fifty to sixty boys, running a fourth-string team against the only opposition in the private school league, a third-string team against a neighboring high school, and either of two nearly equal varsity teams of seven runners each against the best schools in the East, while the other unit took on the West Point plebes and beat them! His runners held unusual distinction among schoolboys and their coaches. On one day in 1959, Robin Lingle, now coaching at the University of Missouri, ran and won two cross-country races over the challenging course at Van Cortlandt Park. Several years later, a pair of Stony Brookers, Peter Randall and Glenn Ogden, startled spectators of a major race at Van Cortlandt Park by tying for first place, while setting a meet record. In recent years, Marve Goldberg has produced not one, not two, but *three* New York State cross-country champions *in the same family*—the Whitneys, Mark and Andy, each of whom won the boys' title in twelfth grade, and their sister Laura, who has won the girls' gold medals in eighth, ninth, and tenth grades, as of this writing.

Several of his protégés have carried on as collegiate champions and All-Americans, AAU titlists and national record-holders. But Marvin Goldberg is just as interested in the also-rans, the boy or girl who never wins a race or even scores a point in competition but who gives everything day after day in practice, who faithfully and uncomplainingly does the work-outs. He also encourages young children by giving them moderate running work-outs, which he carefully supervises with the same attention given to older boys and girls. It's not unusual at a Stony Brook track practice to see a ten-year-old neighborhood boy or an eight-year-old faculty daughter completing a work-out adapted to his or her age and ability.

Perhaps this is what influenced my sons and daughter to

choose track as their major sport—the fact that from the beginning they were never left along the sidelines while the real athletes drilled; instead, they were always made to feel as though
they belonged to the team. As early as Don's tenth birthday, he
was asked by Coach Goldberg if he'd like to run in a three-
quarter-mile cross-country race that Stony Brook's seventh and
eighth graders were running that afternoon. Nobody could have
offered Don a better birthday present! What's more, he won!
Whenever possible, Goldberg arranged for competition that
would encourage and stimulate these younger runners. By the
time they became eligible for high school competition, they'd already gained a sophistication about the sport beyond their years.

With a father like me, so intensely interested in the sport of
track and in their success as runners, my sons' athletics might
have been reduced to an ego-struggle, if I'd been their only
coach. But as it was, I became Marve Goldberg's assistant, with
every confidence in his judgment. I happily turned over the
coaching of my sons to this master. This took some of the natural
heat of a father-son relationship off us all; somebody else was
making the major decisions about our sport. We didn't always
agree. Sometimes as coach-to-coach we'd have to settle a personal problem; sometimes as coach-to-athlete, a few sparks
might fly. But for the most part, we kept the sport where it
belonged, subordinate to our personal courtesy and affection for
each other.

In Marvin Goldberg, his athletes have seen not only an outstanding coach but also a master teacher, a naturalist in the
truest sense of the word. His knowledge of the migratory habits
of a flock of Canada geese or the changing patterns of clouds
could enliven an afternoon's practice session. In the breadth of
his interests—ornithology, geology, meteorology, astronomy, bot-
any, oceanography—he resembles that other naturalist, Henry
David Thoreau, who wrote, "I have travelled a good deal in
Concord." No one would dispute Marve Goldberg's claim to
have done the same in Stony Brook. Certainly no other teacher

would dare to stage his final examination as a walking tour of the campus.

His mastery extends to hobbies and avocations. Driftwood from Long Island's beaches becomes a household ornament after hours of polishing with linseed oil; a patch of soil can blossom into rows of corn; and he has more than a passing interest in railroads and in choral music. But Marvin Goldberg's greatest contribution to those who know him—young and old, athletes and scholars—hasn't been his coaching or teaching, his amazing scope of knowledge or his desire to learn more. In all these has he been exemplary, but in his cheerful refusal to yield to pain or infirmity he has quietly established a lasting standard for Christian character. For in spite of a physical affliction that might level most men, he continues as living proof, to weary cross-country runners and discouraged chemistry students and overburdened faculty colleagues, that we can indeed do all things through Christ.

All along the way, my sons and I have been peculiarly blessed by associating with coaches who were as good to us as fathers, decent men who really cared about their athletes. You don't have to be an athlete yourself, and your son doesn't need to be a star to benefit from knowing men like these and learning from them. Some coaches, however, are also like Gil Dodds and Marvin Goldberg, men who want young people's lives to count for Jesus Christ. St. Paul would have been that kind of coach. In loving concern he demanded the best of the young Christians he was training for the Race of Life. "Do you not know," asked Paul, "that in a race all the runners run, but only one gets the prize? Run in such a way as to get the prize" (1 Corinthians 9:24). That prize Paul refers to is nothing less than God's own summons to excellence, an eternal garland of righteousness. Like those coaches we've known and admired on earth, God the Father also wants us to be better than we are.

CHAPTER 9

Like Father, Like Son

Every father wonders what his little boy will be when he grows up. Some men look at their own lives and see disadvantages or missed opportunities. They say, "I want my son to have it better than I did. I don't want him to make my mistakes." Other men yearn for the same experiences to be repeated in their son's life. At his birth they enroll the newborn in their college; they begin taking their son to work while he's just a toddler; they plan his career, pointing toward the day when he will succeed his dad as chairman of the board. For these men, the fourteenth-century English poet William Langland said it all in *The Vision of Piers Plowman,* when he wrote, "Like father, like son."

In some ways, the old adage is true: I am my father's son and proud of being "a chip off the old block." In physical appearance —facial resemblance, height and weight—to be sure, but also in other ways. My appreciation for history, my delight at hearing and recounting stories or telling jokes are traits identified with my father. They remind all who knew him that I'm unmistakably his son. Unfortunately, the same may be said for some of my less admirable attributes. My impulsive nature, my impatience, my somewhat frenetic tendencies under stress are inherited characteristics whose source I recognize. In attitudes, temperament, and response to most situations, I suppose, I'm a walking example of "like father, like son." Yet in other ways, we have always been different men. If he was Odysseus, then I must have been his son Telemachus. My father remained a wanderer all his life, an alien resident in this country, whereas I became a naturalized

American citizen as soon as legally qualified. There's no question that my father's itchy feet caused a strong counter-reaction in me, probably accounting for my quarter century at Stony Brook. I wanted for my children a quality of living I'd never known— the sense of belonging to somewhere, a hometown they could call their own. Minor differences, perhaps; yet telling, and in their own way an unintentional repudiation of my father's style of life.

Every son must learn to become his own man. Following in his father's footsteps may be a pleasing sentiment, but in time most young men feel a need to blaze their own trails, to set out on their own courses. Going back to the previous chapter for a moment, if fathers are indeed like coaches, then like coaches they too want their young men to exceed the best they themselves have ever done. Walt Whitman wrote, in *Song of Myself,*

I am the teacher of athletes, . . .
He most honors my style who learns under it to destroy the
   teacher.

If a father has done wisely by his children, bringing them up in the training and instruction of the Lord, he ought to have prepared them to assume responsibility for their lives when he can no longer make decisions for them. He ought to have taught them well enough so that they no longer need him to think and act for them. In this respect, the most successful father is the man who's in the process of working himself out of his job. Isn't this the kind of father most of us want to be?

But the real reason why our lives take on different shapes, son from father, lies in our different vocations, our different callings. In my own case, Dad had one vocation, I another. Let me explain. In the sloppy use of language, the word *vocation,* like many words, has lost its primary meaning. It's come to be little more than a synonym for "occupation," mere "employment," a word confused with "job." But to Christians the word *vocation* has a far higher meaning. It derives from the Latin verb *vocare,* "to call," and in Latin grammar the vocative case is used to call someone by name. Remember how, in Shakespeare's play *Julius Caesar*, Mark Antony calls out to "Friends, Romans, countrymen"?

In the New Testament, the Greek word *klēsis* translates into either "vocation" or "calling." St. Paul, who uses the word on numerous occasions, refers both to God's call away from sin and death to righteousness and life as well as to God's calling to a particular station in life, a place of service to him: in other words, a God-ordained vocation. Because it's God's calling, every Christian's vocation is important and should be taken seriously. There's nothing cheap or insignificant about being called by God himself. It's a high and a holy calling, a heavenward calling. As Philip Doddridge wrote, " 'Tis God's all-animating voice/That calls thee from on high." This call is first, an invitation to become his sons and live in obedience to our Heavenly Father; it's also a call to serve him as sons.

God's calling is personal. From Adam in Eden to St. John on Patmos, the Bible tells of God's personally addressing men and women with his call—Enoch, Noah, Abraham, Moses, Ruth, Isaiah, Amos, Mary and Joseph, Matthew the publican and Simon the Zealot, Erastus the politican and Luke the doctor: God calls each of them and us by name. There's nothing vague or uncertain about God's call. It's both a test of willingness and a call to specific action. When the young Isaiah saw his vision of God's holiness and majesty, he was struck down with awe. But God wasn't satisfied with Isaiah's "Woe to me!" God wanted a willing messenger courageous enough to carry a mixed bag of bad news as well as good to the most difficult audience in the world, Isaiah's own people. So God asked, "Whom shall I send? And who will go for us?" Isaiah's response was what God was waiting for: "Here am I. Send me!" (Isaiah 6:1–8).

Obviously, God needs witnesses, and sometimes for special reasons he will call a person out of one profession into a new field of service. The call by Jesus of Nazareth to fishermen to leave their nets and become his apostles is the notable example. But God doesn't call everyone to be a prophet or preacher: in fact, there are few if any specifically "Christian" vocations. Even the Apostle Paul went on making tents for a living, while at the same time fulfilling his apostolic calling. We shouldn't expect God's calling to mean that all truck drivers must give up hauling their rigs to become evangelists. In most cases, God's call to them will say, "Keep on truckin'."

Early in his military career, Lieutenant General William K. Harrison was stationed with a cavalry regiment in the Philippines. Up until that time, he'd never doubted God's vocation for him: He was a soldier, God's man under orders. He'd prepared for his vocation at West Point; after receiving his commission, he'd gone off with the cavalry to serve God by being the best soldier possible. But now, as a young officer overseas, he suddenly realized the enormous need to evangelize the world for Jesus Christ. Should he resign his commission and become a foreign missionary? Was that really God's call to him? Wasn't there, perhaps, some higher vocation awaiting him than merely being an officer in the United States Army? While he pondered these questions, Harrison recalls, "The Lord led me as clearly as can be to read 1 Corinthians 12:29, which says, 'Are all apostles? Are all prophets? Are all teachers? Do all work miracles?' I knew the answer to those questions, and I also knew what God was telling me. So I stayed on as a soldier." In God's own wisdom, he may allow us—like General Harrison—to confirm our calling, and in his providence he fulfills his divine will in that calling. If Harrison had become a missionary, he'd have been effective, no doubt. What mattered, however, was his willingness to answer God's call.

The rule given by St. Paul to the Corinthians seems clear:

Nevertheless, each one should retain the place in life that the Lord assigned to him and to which God has called him. . . . Each one should remain in the situation which he was in when God called him. . . . Brothers, each man, as responsible to God, should remain in the situation God called him to (1 Corinthians 7:17, 20, 24).

Commenting on this passage, Leon Morris writes, "In passing it is worth noticing that this principle is still valid. Conversion is not the signal for a man to leave his occupation (unless it is one plainly incompatible with Christianity) and seek some other. All of life is God's." Of course, if a man is a pimp or a hit man for the Mafia, a gossip columnist or an expert in political dirty tricks, when God saves him he also gives him a new vocation. But if his work is honorable, his new relationship with God through Christ only enhances the work he's already doing. He becomes a better lawyer or lumberjack because he now works for God and not only for the boss, the paycheck, or his own ego.

As fathers teaching our sons about their life's work and the meaning of God's call, we can assure them of this fact: God never calls us and then fails to use us. We're not like the scrubs on a football team who sit on the bench for the whole season and never get a single minute of playing time. When God decides that we're ready for action, he puts us into the game. In General Harrison's case, he seemed to sit on the sidelines for many years, holding routine assignments in the army, rising slowly through the military ranks. But God knew that the time would come when he'd need someone to be his instrument in resolving the Korean War. General Harrison proved to be that man, as Senior Delegate for the United Nations Command, negotiating the armistice at Panmunjom. This was his specific service in response to God's vocation for him.

Yes, God's call is always to service, never to spectatorship. It's always a summons to action. "Follow me" is Jesus Christ's first command; then "Go!" The clarity and direction of that second command depend upon our obedience to the first, but wherever we're sent to serve, we may be certain of this: God calls us to joyful service, using those very gifts already entrusted to us. This is a wonderfully liberating truth that I want to deal with more personally later in this chapter. Just now, let's think of how a father can help his son to find and realize his own vocation.

First, it's essential to understand that everyone has a vocation, a calling from God. This calling, however, seldom comes to us by means of a heavenly public address system, like Bill Cosby's God speaking to Noah; it may not even be perceived through a still, small voice. But assurance of our proper vocation becomes certain as we learn more about ourselves and our particular gifts. God has endowed each of us with physical and intellectual capabilities, with emotional and spiritual qualities. Along with these he's given us preferences, affinities, likes and dislikes. Some of us are good at numbers and abstract numerical concepts; others are better with words and verbal skills of expression; still others have mechanical abilities or social graces or special insight into human nature or talents for making music or other art. These are God's gifts, spoken of repeatedly in the New Testament letters. They come directly from God and can never be discounted because, as St. Paul writes, "God's gifts and his call are irrevocable" (Romans 11:29). So, if someone is looking for his vocation, he has only to ask himself, "What am I good at doing? What do I enjoy doing?" In all probability, that's his calling, and he can serve God by doing precisely what he does best and most enjoys doing.

Here's where a lot of us have been misguided in our teaching about knowing the will of God for our lives. As a result, some of us have misled our children also. We've always heard that surrendering to God means being willing to do whatever he commands, go wherever he sends. Back of that idea is the nagging fear that God will call us to do something unpleasant. But God doesn't work that way. Hard tasks, yes; challenging mountains to scale, certainly. But whatever God calls us to do, he'll reward us for doing with joy that stamps his approval on our service. True, God sometimes has to convince us by overcoming our natural reluctance, our failure to perceive some hidden talent. God had to twist Moses' arm—at least, make it leprous and then whole again—to convince Moses of his vocation, but that's an exception. If you faint at the sight of blood, God won't necessarily call you to be a surgeon; or if he does, he'll also give you power to overcome your queasy stomach.

As your children mature and begin to pay some attenton to

what their father does for a living, they'll be able to judge for themselves whether or not your work is done with joy or as an act of drudgery. They'll determine whether or not their father's labor is treated as service to God, carrying its own reward, or is he simply doing his job? Is he exemplifying the dignity of all work and the value of money fairly earned? If he's only punching the time clock, he can't be fulfilling God's call, because St. Paul has told us regarding our daily toil, "Whatever you do, work at it with all your heart, as working for the Lord, not for men" (Colossians 3:23). Children will reach these conclusions on the basis of what they observe as you leave home for work in the morning and return at the end of the day. They'll judge by your attitude toward their mother and themselves. A man who hates his work is seldom happy at home either. On the other hand, a man whose work means more to him than his family has confused his priorities: his vocation has become his obsession.

Here's where I have to be careful. I love to write. I can be perfectly contented spending a dozen hours a day at the typewriter. I used to feel that every arrival home—my wife from her work as a teacher, our sons or daughter from school—represented an intrusion upon my work. As the door opened, I'd call out a sort of disgruntled "Hello," whose tone said, "Don't bother me, I'm busy!" But repeated instances of disappointment, crossed wires, and failure to communicate have finally taught me a lesson: *My family is more important than my work.* They aren't intruding on my private sanctuary; they're returning home. If I really love them as I claim, then I gladly give them my time and attention.

My son Don clinched this lesson for me one day by insisting that I listen to a recording of a song by Sandy and Harry Chapin called "Cat's in the Cradle." This song is a warning to every father who's too busy for what matters most.

It's no good trying to excuse ourselves on the grounds that we're working for the family's well-being. They won't accept that argument. Yes, it's great if we can provide our wife and children with the comforts of home, but what they really want is us, not just what our hard work can buy. That's been a lesson well worth applying, and I'm grateful to the Chapins for teaching it. Too bad it took me so long to learn. Nowadays, I welcome my family home. When I hear someone's arrival, I shut off the electric typewriter, rise from my desk, and go out of my study to greet whoever's at the door. After a few moments, I may return to write some more; or I may call it a day, grateful to spend the remaining hours with my family.

We can't get away, either, with blaming God for our misplaced values. No matter how earnestly I'm trying to serve God in my vocation—whether as a writer or policeman or accountant or evangelist—if I neglect my duties as a husband and father, I invalidate my work. I can't serve God without serving those people whom God has entrusted to my care. Unless our children, not to mention our wives, can see that our work is kept in its proper perspective, they'll resent what we do. No amount of sweet talk about its importance to God will convince them, if they're being shortchanged. Instead of robbing my family, my work ought to make me a better father, a better husband. A man called by God to joyful service feasts on a banquet of inner contentment, a cornucopia of blessings to be shared with his loved ones. As a father, in particular, the effect of my attitudes toward my work influences any decision my son will make about his vocation. Much of his own choice to respond to God's call will be determined by what he's seen in me.

But we also need to remind ourselves of whose vocation it's to be. Not mine, but his, my son's vocation. I have mine, for which I thank God: but that's my calling. I can't assume that, just because my children have grown up in the home of a father who's a writer and teacher, a mother who's a nurse and teacher, any of them will be called to the same vocation. Is today supposed to be the same as yesterday? I must know my own vocation and go to work each day convinced that what I'm doing is in direct response to God's call to me. But I must also leave to God how, when, and to what work he will call my sons and daughter.

This was a problem between my father and me. He had his firm ideas of what God would call me to do; I resisted Dad's pressure. Our situation wasn't unusual. As Samuel Johnson told Boswell, "There must always be a struggle between a father and son, while one aims at power and the other at independence." But to be fair to my father, his motives weren't simply to control my life but to expand his own. Ever since he'd been forced by ill health to leave his Northern Ontario mission church, Ernie Lockerbie had felt incomplete. He wanted to serve God in hard places; the persons he most admired were pioneer missionaries— Mary Slessor of Calabar, Adoniram Judson of Burma, David Brainerd among the American Indians. Their biographies held a prominent position on his library shelves. His sermons drew upon illustrations from their lives. His heart belonged to foreign missions.

For several years after World War II, my father ceased to be a local pastor. Instead, he traveled across North America as a deputation secretary for mission societies working with the world's most desperately needy people, its ten or twelve million lepers. In those days, more so perhaps than today, the largest Canadian and American churches concentrated much of their missions' emphases into two-week extravaganzas called "missionary conferences." The great ones still continue at the Park Street Church in Boston, at Highland Park Baptist Church in Southfield, Michigan, and elsewhere. These conventions promoted a variety of missionary work, with rosters of distinguished speakers. But for me the main feature was never the oral addresses nor even the slides and soundless motion pictures, narrated by a ghostly voice at the screen; for me the highlight would always be the display booths and their curios calculated to dramatize the most exotic elements of foreign missionary life. Here one could see shrunken heads, pagan charms and fetishes, or pygmy blowguns. Here one could stand next to the great missionary statesmen and pioneers, listening at close range to stories of how they'd survived harrowing encounters with witch doctors and cannibals, wild beasts and rare diseases. Who were these giants of courage and commitment? Rowland V. Bingham of Africa, Jonathan Goforth of China, Silas Fox of India, among others.

I thrilled at knowing that my father stood among them all, even though he had never crossed their oceans or trekked among their tribes. He was nonetheless their deputy at home, making possible by his efforts wider support in prayer and money so that their work might flourish. For him, as for them, foreign missions meant heeding a cry for help from people who had never heard the message of salvation through Jesus Christ. My father believed passionately that the heathen were lost—no equivocation about it, no blasphemous talk about *apokatastasis,* or universal salvation. The truth for him had been expressed in the words of Dr. A. B. Simpson, patriarch of the Christian and Missionary Alliance:

A hundred thousand souls a day are passing one by one away
In Christless guilt and gloom . . .
They're passing to their doom.

My father and his colleagues lifted their voices in this *dies irae,* warning of God's impending and implacable Day of Wrath. I too sang the tune, thumping out its rhythms like "The Song of the Volga Boatmen."

The Mount Everest of all missionary conferences, then as now, came each spring in Toronto at The Peoples' Church. Its pastor was Dr. Oswald J. Smith, a scrawny, hawk-faced man with tics of hypertension. Smith's own preaching abilities seemed negligible, although that scarcely mattered. Indeed, while living in Toronto and attending The Peoples' Church from 1946 through 1948, I rarely heard Smith preach at all. But he had two greater gifts, one of which was a talent for writing simple yet original lyrics for gospel songs. Today Smith's best known songs may be "There Is Joy in Serving Jesus," "Saved, Saved, Saved," or "Into the Heart of Jesus."

Oswald J. Smith's other gift was his skill at impelling his congregation and its satellites to give hundreds of thousands of dollars to missions. One of his slogans, borrowed from Charles Haddon Spurgeon and often repeated in my hearing, was this: "If God calls you to be a missionary, don't stoop to become a king!"

Another of his sayings was, "Why should anyone hear the Gospel twice until everyone has heard it once?"

His method of fund raising was to take pledges or "faith promises" of so-many dollars per month. Smith's means of motivation were many. For visual incentive, he displayed a tall pasteboard thermometer with a moveable red ribbon aiming upward toward the sum of money marking that year's goal. Smith's appeal to nationalism egged on his Canadian congregation with threats that this year Dr. Harold John Ockenga and his Park Street Church were out to beat The Peoples' Church in total giving to missions. "But," Smith would snarl, "the Americans didn't beat us in the War of 1812, and they won't beat us today!" The usually staid Canadian audience would cheer and applaud as if at a political rally. Smith's final appeal would be eschatological. By our giving to missions, he assured us, we could actually influence God's timetable and hasten the day of the Lord's return. Even now, thirty years later, I find myself baffled but intrigued by Oswald J. Smith's argument.

Every mission society in North America yearned for a place in The Peoples' Church conference, preferably as close to its end as possible. Every year that climax came on Easter Sunday. All that day Smith would be even more nervous than usual, fidgeting in his platform chair, timing each speaker to the second with a red light on the pulpit to signal that his allotted time had expired. God help the hundred thousand souls in your part of the world if you dared to go on speaking past your time! Smith would bound forward out of his chair and all but shove the next speaker to the front, scorching the offender with a baleful look that sentenced him never to be invited to return. Only the strong survived. The secret was to capture Smith's attention the first time you spoke.

E. A. Lockerbie made it his business to get and hold Oswald J. Smith's approval. While other representatives were quietly making their way to the microphone, using up precious seconds, my father would begin to speak at the instant his time began, from wherever he was standing on the platform, ignoring any need for the public address system, raising his voice to a volume that could be heard throughout the huge auditorium, compressing his entire presentation into one vivid, unforgettable scene. Of course, my father knew he had two advantages over other missionary spokesmen. First, his work was fascinating to an audience in much the same way that a bloody highway wreck compels other drivers to gawk. Dad's horrifying portraits of disfigured and suffering victims of Hansen's Disease (as modern medicine prefers to call leprosy) lingered in the minds of his listeners. Second, E. A. Lockerbie was still a salesman. Whether badgering, cajoling, or challenging, he was all the time slipping his foot in the door. It was almost unfair to see what he could do to the competition. Some speakers who found themselves scheduled to speak on the same occasion would literally appeal to be rescheduled at a time when they didn't have to face the prospect of being overwhelmed by Lockerbie and his lepers. As for Dad, he loved every minute of it!

In 1951, after five years on the road, my father resumed being a pastor. He now made foreign missions the first priority of his new pastorate, without question hoping to emulate Oswald J. Smith. From the seed planted by E. A. Lockerbie's vision for foreign missions sprang up a bumper crop of volunteers, including his own daughter, my sister Jeannie, some three years younger than I. Jeannie has been, quite literally, a missionary all her life. As a little girl in third grade, she began a weekly Bible story club for neighborhood playmates, meeting in the basement of our Toronto home. As an early teenager, she worked in a summer camp sponsored by a Christian mission evangelizing among New York City's Jews. From the time she entered high school, she seemed always to know that she would become a missionary nurse. At Brooklyn's Methodist Hospital, where Lory also was a nursing student, and later in college, she prepared specifically to join Dr. Viggo Olsen and his wife Joan at Memorial Christian Hospital in Malumghat, Bangladesh. In 1963, she sailed to what was then called East Pakistan, working first in medicine and more recently in literature translation and publications.

One of my father's happiest moments was the occasion of my

parents' visit to see their daughter and her work among the Bengali people. Ten years later, my family also journeyed to Golden Bengal, visiting with Jeannie and her colleagues, sharing briefly in what is for them a life-long calling. Only three months earlier, Jeannie and I had stood by our father's grave in the Hudson Valley of New York State. Now we joined in singing a duet in far-off Bangladesh, lifting up the exultant words of one of Ernie Lockerbie's favorite hymns:

> O happy day that fixed my choice
> On Thee, my Saviour and my God!
> Well may this glowing heart rejoice,
> And tell its raptures all abroad.

But I was only a visitor at Malumghat and Chittagong; not quite a tourist, but certainly not a missionary either. In those days of viewing my sister's work, I felt once more the sting of my father's reproach; for, while recognizing the many ways in which I seemed to be so different from him, he had nonetheless always yearned for me to fulfill his one great aspiration, to be a foreign missionary. If that was not to be, then at least I should join him as the perennial preacher's kid, the pastor's son, assistant to my father, then successor to his pulpit. He saw us ministering jointly as a team to some great congregation, imitating the roles of The Peoples' Church patriarch and his son, Paul B. Smith.

For a brief time only, during the summer of 1956, between my university graduation and the beginning of my first teaching appointment, my father had seen his dream take shape. We worked together to begin rebuilding a faltering congregation in a stately old inner-city church. In those few weeks the crowds began to return from the suburbs, won by the power of his preaching. My responsibilities were to direct the choir and prepare the weekly radio broadcast; but Dad also insisted that I appear with him, Sunday by Sunday, on the platform to read the Scripture or lead the congregational singing, to make announcements or, on occasion, attempt to preach myself. Didn't he know how ill at ease I felt, how out of place, how mortified by his fulsome praise? I knew then that I wasn't cut out for the pastorate, that I'd never be able to fulfill my father's dream.

The fact is that I owe it largely to men other than my father that I was able to discern my own vocation at all. In my senior year at New York University, I was still terribly uncertain about my future. With a major in English and a minor in religious studies, I had in mind some sort of ministry; but where to go for further study was a big question. My father favored a denominational institution calling itself a seminary when, in reality, it was only a Bible institute; few of its students had more than a high school diploma, and so it was hardly a seminary in the graduate school sense of the name. Its dean was Dr. John R. Dunkin, whom I'd known in London, Ontario, when he was the pastor of Wortley Road Baptist Church. I decided to ask his advice.

At the same time, my undergraduate advisor in religious studies at New York University had been urging me to look farther afield. Professor Robert Perry had been a catalyst to my growth throughout my years at NYU—the first person who ever challenged me to read the Bible carefully, to see past my literalism to the wealth of meanings in Scripture. An ordained Presbyterian minister, Robert Perry's ideas about the Bible and Christianity at first scalded my conscience. I'll never forget one of the early questions he asked me. "Do you believe the Bible word-for-word?" Naturally, I assured him that I did. "Then what does it mean, in Genesis 3, when it says that 'God walked in the garden in the cool of the day'? Does God have legs?" Put in this present context, the question now seems silly, inconsequential, but it was anything but silly or insincere at that time. Robert Perry knew precisely the kind of student he had before him—a captious, contentious, and essentially uncritical freshman, so bound down by what he'd heard about the Bible that he'd never had to bother reading it intelligently.

To their credit, both these men—though different in their theology—dealt honestly with me. John Dunkin, visiting our home one weekend, told me directly that, while he'd welcome my presence at his institution, going there wasn't the logical step to follow a university education. Instead, he recommended the Graduate School at Wheaton College in Illinois or Dallas Theological Seminary in Texas. For his part, Professor Perry at first urged me to apply for scholarships at two liberal seminaries in Hartford and Chicago; after I was awarded these scholarships, however, he changed his mind, telling me, "You'd be better off where people believe more like you do." I honor both men for their integrity.

I went to Wheaton. In mid-summer the English Department chairman, Dr. Clyde S. Kilby, offered me a teaching position to go along with my theological studies in the graduate school. Clyde Kilby is one of the dearest, wisest souls I've ever known. He took me on when all I knew about the teaching of English to college freshmen and sophomores could have been inscribed on a pinhead. Nonetheless he stuck by me, encouraging me to begin corollary graduate work in English, prompting me to become involved as a full member of the faculty, urging me to participate in professional meetings and even to submit my puerile writings for publication. At the same time that I was beginning my long devotion to Clyde Kilby, I was also working with Gil Dodds in coaching track; thus I had the benefit of learning from two masters at once.

After having been away from home for less than three months, I returned at Thanksgiving. Lory and I were to be married in three weeks' time, and I was full of those prospects. But I also had much to tell my parents about the remarkable opportunity I was experiencing at Wheaton, for I was receiving practical exposure to five different vocations at once: teaching English to college freshmen and sophomores, studying theology, coaching track while continuing to compete myself, assisting in a church's choral and youth programs, and also speaking on the circuit of youth rallies, where an athlete is often a popular attraction. In addition, my first published article was about to appear in a magazine. By a process of concrete experience, I was becoming aware of God's call to joyful service—not as a pastor or youth evangelist or minister of music; not even as a college track coach, glamorous as I'd once thought that might be. I would be, instead, a teacher and writer.

But I remember that Thanksgiving holiday with regret largely because of my father's disappointment in me. He'd seen the dissolving of his dream as he heard me tell of my elation at knowing God's call. But because that choice of vocation did not appear to be sending me overseas as a missionary, nor even delivering me over to him as a perpetual assistant pastor, he felt cheated. His parting words to me at the airport conveyed his desperation. He gripped my shoulders with both hands and, shaking his head from side to side, said mournfully, "And to think, I remember the time you dedicated your life to be a missionary to Russia!"

It was true. As a child of twelve at one of those many missionary conferences, I had heard Peter Deyneka's powerful appeal. This little man, whom Oswald J. Smith called "Peter Dynamite," had painted indelibly in my mind a picture of spiritual famine in the Soviet Union; he had challenged us to carry the Gospel to Russia. I had responded publicly, knowing little or nothing about the Kremlin's reluctance to issue visas to Christian missionaries. Now, a decade later, in the depths of the Cold War— Richard Nixon's "kitchen debate" and Nikita Sergeyevich Khrushchev's promise to bury the West—I was being held accountable for failing to evangelize Mother Russia! I stiffened against my father's hold and spun away without another word to board my plane. Years later, he remembered that I had uttered no reply and claimed it as proof that my choice of vocation had been contrary to God's will for my life.

To my knowledge, my father never reconciled himself to accepting that God's call for me was to be a teacher and writer; but all that is behind us now. Dad has entered into the splendors of God's eternity, while I'm still at work here for my allotted time. I've told you all this about my father and me because, for better and for worse, I am who I am because of him; whatever I know about being a father, I first learned from him. Perhaps he never knew how much I loved him. Probably in the thirty-seven years of our lives together, I never quite realized how much he cared for me either. For this, I must accept my share of the blame because my father was a warmhearted man, a person whose compassion and affection for others I haven't yet fully learned to emulate.

Midway through that year at Wheaton, on December 15, 1956, Lory and I were married in the Bay Ridge Baptist Church, where we'd first met four years earlier. Dad had introduced us, and it was his joy to officiate at our wedding ceremony. I took Lory to Pinecrest Farms, outside of Wheaton, where Harry and Esther Duncan were more than landlords to us; they were like father and mother. Harry counseled this male chauvinist bridegroom in the care and treatment of women. Esther helped Lory prepare her first casserole for an English Department potluck supper and comforted her during my frequent weekend absences to run in track meets on the East Coast circuit. From them both we learned that love is more than passion and marriage a great deal more than living together.

But sooner than we'd expected, Lory became pregnant. The apartment we rented in the Duncans' farmhouse had no space for a nursery; reluctantly, we faced the prospect of moving. About this same time, I asked Clyde Kilby if it would be appropriate to discuss my future at Wheaton. He invited me to his home one evening, and after his wife Martha had served us tea, we talked about my prospects. He was in the middle of describing an attractive appointment for the following year when he interrupted himself. "I don't want you to think I'm at all eager to lose you, Bruce, but I've just thought of something that might interest you. I received a phone call today from Frank Gaebelein at The Stony Brook School on Long Island. He was calling to ask me if we have a graduating senior who might be a candidate for a position at his school." As Kilby went on to reconstruct his conversation with the Stony Brook headmaster, I began to feel an eerie glow of certainty that he was speaking prophetically about me. Stony Brook was looking not only for an English teacher but also for someone who could take charge of choral music and possibly assist in athletics. I drove back to Pinecrest Farms that night with news that I felt sure would please my bride: If the Lord willed, we'd be going back to New York.

We met Dr. Frank E. Gaebelein in April of 1957 and accepted his offer to come to Stony Brook for the following September. It was the beginning of my career, the true beginning of our life together in the place we would always consider to be home. At Stony Brook we found a community, people committed to working with teenagers (boys only until 1971) and pointing them toward the Person of Jesus Christ. We found other young couples like ourselves just starting out: Bruce and Carolyn Dodd, who delivered our baby Ellyn; Terry and Andrea Harrison; our present headmaster, Karl Soderstrom, and his wife Jean; people idealistic as we were, impoverished as we were, willing to help each other. As our children grew, we often remarked that they had many parents, many adults who cared for them and about them. We were poor, we were frequently in doubt about the future, but we stayed and stayed and stayed.

My principal reason for remaining at Stony Brook lay in the presence and example of Frank E. Gaebelein. He'd been Stony Brook's only headmaster since 1922; in thirty-five years, the school had grown from two dozen boys to nearly two hundred. Its scope had broadened from being an educational oddity—a college-preparatory school with Bible teaching at the heart of its curriculum—to being the model for many such schools. Under God, Frank Gaebelein had been responsible for this leadership through his preaching and lectures, but also through the influence of his books. In spite of the demands of boarding school administration, Dr. Gaebelein had published several books on biblical studies and education, including two enduring volumes, *Christian Education in a Democracy* and *The Pattern of God's Truth*. But Frank Gaebelein was no ivory-tower pedant. He lived his life among boys, eating often in the Stony Brook dining room, playing informal piano recitals for groups of students in his living room, taking a daily and astonishingly brisk walk around the campus to keep himself fit for his summer mountaineering, cheering Stony Brook's teams at all levels of competition, counseling boys at all hours of the day and night.

I saw in this man a fullness of life and experience that appealed to me, for with all his manifold accomplishments, Frank Gaebelein remained a humble and caring man, responsive to the needs of this young, impulsive teacher. With tact and grace he began to motivate me to attempt some serious writing of my own; when I did, he insisted on seeing my rough drafts and going over them like a Cambridge don. He was solicitous not only of making my prose of publishable quality but also of maintaining the good name of the school. "We must never allow anything to go out under a Stony Brook byline that suggests carelessness or shoddy thinking," Gaebelein told me more than once. His review of my work delved far below the surface level of my argument; he talked to me about verbal precision, about the power of an active verb to sweep away mounds of adjectives and adverbs. "I had a teacher," he told me, "who used to praise my *ease* and *elegance,* but she was wrong. The very qualities she praised were what I had to learn to overcome in writing." Little by little, Frank Gaebelein pruned my prose, rooting out my weedlike superfluity of language, editing down my overblown descriptions until nothing remained but a lean noun and a vivid verb.

He taught me by precept. As a boy at Mount Vernon High School, he'd been a classmate of E. B. White and recommended for my own use White's edition of William Strunk's little classic, *The Elements of Style.* Frank Gaebelein also taught by example. His own sermons, even his brief Wednesday evening Bible lessons, were models of preparation both in study and in expression. His articles and essays likewise practised what he preached. In time, he turned me loose from his literary scrutiny, although never from the power of his standards. I make no pretense of having attained to his level of mastery in writing English sentences, but the day came when I knew that I'd won his respect and confidence when he told me that he'd recommended me to write a book about The Stony Brook School. That book, *The*

Way They Should Go, could never have been written without his willingness to open his memory and his files, to subject himself to criticism. Thus, even after Frank Gaebelein had ceased to be my tutor, he continued to be a fatherly example of Christian maturity.

As I was helped to know my vocation by the concern of men like Frank Gaebelein, so God has given me these years at Stony Brook in which to encourage young people in their search to know God's calling for them. Some of them have been boys from ordinary homes with ordinary expectations—to get a job, to make a lot of money, to be successful. I've never hesitated to show that there may be more to life than those narrow goals suggest; that education is more than the acquiring of career skills. Once in a while, this teaching has imbedded itself in a boy's soul and changed his life's direction. Other boys are also from ordinary homes but come blessed by extraordinary energy, industry, imagination, and a healthy ambition. They arrive at school in ninth or tenth grade and light up an English classroom with their eagerness to learn everything about anything. For them, my work is little more than maintaining what their parents have already instilled, a joy in learning and a desire to share that knowledge with the rest of the world.

Over the years a few boys have been the sons of famous men—politicians and pastors, corporation executives and evangelists, opera stars and missionaries, college presidents and diplomats. Their fathers' names are household words, and often these boys seem borne down by the weight of their fathers' renown. Ben Jonson said, "Greatness of name in the father ofttimes overwhelms the son; they stand too near one another. The shadow kills the growth." Furthermore, in spite of having enjoyed every advantage our society can afford, some of these boys are lacking the one thing their schoolmates from obscure families possess—a sure sense of a father's continuing presence and concern. In almost every case, the kindest thing to be done for them is to allow them anonymity and the opportunity to forget just who their fathers are. In time, as their confidence grows, these boys come to realize that nobody really cares about their fathers; we're more interested in their own merits as persons.

Sometimes one's apparent effect upon a boy is almost nonexistent; at most, it may be indirect until God, in his own time, gets hold of that person's life. Some of my students, whose writing left my eyes bloodshot and bleary, are now themselves resourceful writers, teachers of composition and literature. Others whose rebelliousness against God or any other authority seemed to destine them for short, unhappy lives are now pastors or missionaries, leaders in their churches and communities. You can never predict what a boy's eventual vocation will be.

A couple of years ago, after I'd finished speaking in a chapel service at Geneva College in Beaver Falls, Pennsylvania, a young woman I didn't know approached and introduced herself as the wife of a former Stony Brook student. "Do you remember Jeff?" she asked, a little tentatively. Did I remember Jeff! One of the all-time hell-raisers! "He's finishing up his student teaching this semester, and he asked me to make an appointment for him. He'd like to see you." We arranged a time that same afternoon. Jeff and his wife came together, and he told me his story.

He'd come to Stony Brook from a supposedly religious home, but none of our teaching had registered with him. "Chapel services were just like water rolling off a duck's back," he said, "and I just never believed what I heard in Bible class." He only prayed once, the night he got caught drunk and was propped up in a cold shower in the infirmary. "As my head cleared, I remember saying out loud, 'O God, help me not to become an alcoholic.'" Later on, Jeff was expelled from Stony Brook for repeated violation of school rules; then he was kicked out of his next school and recommended for psychiatric care. "My doctor wasn't a Christian," Jeff says, "but he suggested that I read the Book of Proverbs as part of my therapy. I still had my Stony Brook textbooks, including the Bible, and I used that. But one night, I reached for the Bible and missed. What came off the shelf was a copy of *The Pilgrim's Progress* that you tried to teach me in tenth grade." The book fell open to the place where Faithful tells Christian about his pilgrimage. As Jeff read, he felt his own need of Jesus Christ and prayed for salvation right there and then. Today, Jeff is teaching sixth grade in a Christian school.

Now the passing years have brought my own sons to that time in their lives when they too must hear and respond to the call of God. How will they serve him? Who will help them to know God's will for their lives? It's obviously too soon to say that they know their vocations, but interestingly enough, each has chosen to work for the time being with men who were once my younger colleagues at Stony Brook—men whose own direction God gave me a small part in shaping. So the spiral of influence winds on, each of us bound more tightly to the other than we'll ever know. The poet and priest John Donne wrote, "No man is an island, entire of itself"; then he said, "I am involved in mankind." This is another way of expressing what St. Paul means when he says, "Carry each other's burdens, and in this way you will fulfill the law of Christ" (Galatians 6:2). To care for my own sons is essential; but to care about another man's son, without intruding on that father's prerogatives—to become *involved:* That's what it means to "fulfill the law of Christ."

CHAPTER 10

Faith of Our Fathers

Charles Manson, imprisoned cult leader and mass murderer, still receives hundreds of letters from young people wanting to know how to join his "family." Manson himself doesn't know why they write to him. According to Los Angeles radio station KNX, however, Manson supposes that parents aren't giving their children anything to believe in, and so these children are looking desperately for something to commit themselves to.

Bizarre as it seems, this news shouldn't shock us. We live in an era when our children and we have been victimized by one disappointment after another. Our heroes seem to be in short supply, and many of those we once looked to have turned out to be failing idols—greedy, corrupt, far less admirable than we'd imagined. Scandals in politics, embezzlement in charities, strikes by doctors and firemen, cheating at West Point, games fixed by pro athletes, adultery in churches: Whom can you trust nowadays? Cynicism prevails, creating a vacuum of disbelief in anything worthwhile, including religious faith.

Among some experts on child-rearing a notion prevails which they pass on to their disciples: Children ought to be shielded from any adult pressure regarding religion. Many parents go along with this advice, especially if they're reacting against a negative experience in their own childhood. "I was brought up in a home," says Ron, "where all my parents did was fight about religion. My mother was a devout Roman Catholic; my father was a Baptist, only he didn't go to church very much. But every row they ever had seemed to be over which religion was right.

As soon as I could, I stopped going to church myself, and I decided I wouldn't burden my kids with any of that business either. So Nancy and I don't ever mention religion to our kids. So far as I'm concerned, they can take it or leave it."

Ron is sincere; yet as his children grow, will his sincerity be sufficient to nourish them? Or will they, like so many others, look for something else to satisfy the hunger they feel, to fill the void within? As we know, nature abhors a vacuum; it must be filled by something, even if that something appals. Boys and girls who are permitted the apparent luxury of growing up with no religious instruction—no Sunday School or confirmation classes, no Christian Service Brigade or Pioneer Girls, no Vacation Bible School or summer camps like Deerfoot Lodge or Tapawingo—have been robbed by their parents. When they realize that they are spiritual paupers, the unwitting victims of benign neglect, these are the children who rebel most strongly against their parents. They become easy prey for mind-control cults and fanaticism, attracted by the madness and bestiality of a Charles Manson or of the Symbionese Liberation Army, by a Hell's Angels motorcycle gang or even by a Satanic coven.

Why do these hoodlums and cults hold such fascination for our youth? Because they offer precisely what's been missing in the upbringing of so many children—a spiritual commitment to something more valuable than material goods and well-being. No wonder Jewish leaders in America, like Rabbis Marc Tannenbaum and Balfour Brickner, have recently been warning irreligious families who no longer profess to believe in the God of Abraham, Isaac, and Jacob. By ignoring their children's religious heritage, these parents are abandoning their children to the ravages of the secular wilderness. For make sure of this: Every child puts his faith in someone. If not in God the Father, then in some other god; if not Manson, then Marx, or Moon or some other messiah.

Strangely, some parents and their gurus haven't understood this message. "Let a child make up his own mind," parents are advised. In and of itself, that's perfect sense; indeed, there's no other way for anyone to express personal faith in God except as a result of making up one's own mind. But the flaw in such advice is the idea that children need no exposure to religious teaching and no example of commitment in order to make up their minds. Nothing could be farther from the truth. What makes us suppose that today's child, left to his own choice, will learn to appreciate Beethoven as well as the Bee Gees? What makes us think that a child mesmerized by television's hypnotic appeal will turn away to read the Great Books of the Western World? Or that a child will discover for himself the nourishment of a spinach salad, an omelette, or even a sirloin steak in place of junk food? Left to roam the aisles of a supermarket, most children would fill their shopping carts with candy bars and jellybeans. What makes us any more optimistic about the same child's spiritual diet?

As fathers, the first gift we must give our children is a loving family. Our sons and daughters need assurance that their mother is the most important woman in the world; and along with this assurance, the certainty that they are loved equally and unfailingly. This is the keystone to a child's security. But growing directly from an environment of family love and stability must come another gift supremely necessary, the gift of faith. Not faith as some kind of emotional or psychological abstraction; not faith as a slogan or pep talk—"Keep the faith, baby!"—not faith in America or faith in democracy or faith in ourselves. The only kind of faith that counts, the only real faith possible, is faith in God. The product of a loving, caring Christian family should be the faith we hold in common; a believing trust in the One who made us, who redeems us from sin, who wants to claim us for himself through all eternity. Children should learn about this faith primarily at home from their parents, secondarily at church, and possibly at school, but a father must be the priest in his own home, setting an example of faith for his entire household.

What should be the marks of a Christian father? Church leadership? A reputation for integrity in business? Recognition—possibly even renown—as a spokesman for Jesus Christ? All of these are estimable qualities. If a man is granted Christian maturity and spiritual insight, he should make himself available to serve in his local church as elder or deacon, as trustee or vestryman; he should be willing to be an usher or member of the choir or Sunday School teacher or youth activities sponsor. He should certainly be known as an honest workman, a professional whose word can be trusted, a skilled laborer whose craftsmanship reflects his best efforts. If given the opportunity to reach beyond the limits of his own locality, as a speaker or writer, he must not shun the call of God.

But being a Baptist deacon or an Episcopal senior warden doesn't necessarily make a man the ideal Christian father. Membership in the local chapter of Christian Businessmen International or The Gideons isn't enough of itself. Appearing on "The 700 Club" or preaching to stadiums full of converts doesn't do the job either. It's no news to anyone that some of the most rebellious sons have had fathers who were preachers, evangelists, Christian celebrities. One night, in 1968, I answered a knock at my front door. There stood a former student, twice over our leading scholar at Stony Brook, now enrolled at an Ivy League university. He looked bedraggled and distraught, and as I welcomed him into the house, he told me his story. His father, a household name as a Christian layman, had cut him off, refusing to pay his college bills or offer any further support because this boy had dared to oppose his father's political preference in the Presidential election of that year. The father was willing to alienate his son for the sake of party politics. The boy had come back to his old school that night looking for some counsel, some comfort—looking for a father.

No, appearances aren't enough. To be a Christian father, a man's life must bear witness to his faith in the place where it counts most, his own home. His example must include a living lesson in what it means to be a man of faith wherever and whenever: at home as well as at church, in the community, or at a dis-

tant resort; in momentary excitement or in dull routine, in times
of joy, in times of sorrow.

Of course, the Christian father sees to it that his family attends
church regularly to receive the benefits of instruction, the encouragement of fellowship, the inspiration of worship, the blessings of service. Through the church's inculcation—by preaching,
teaching, and ritual—his children may form patterns of thought
and behavior which later find expression in their own personal
faith. But at home, by prayer and Bible study together as a family, a father reinforces the preaching, teaching, and ritual of the
church. Furthermore, by the daily living out of those doctrines
and creeds, a father teaches much more. His children learn that
the Christian faith is a day-by-day adventure with God, not just
a weekly observance in a sanctuary.

Genuine faith calls for more than Sunday-go-to-meeting religion. It demands an integrated life, a whole experience with
Jesus Christ, centered in him and radiating outward to include
every human relationship. Living in faith doesn't require some
kind of unearthly spirituality; it does require that our humanness
be given over in service to our Maker and Redeemer. These bodies in which we've been formed by God's own pleasure; these
emotions, these minds made new by the presence of the Holy
Spirit; these are the very instruments by which we can serve
God. So, every loving concern, every loving thought, and every
loving act done out of selflessness and regard for others becomes
a sign of God's love working through us; in other words, a sacrament of something holy. Washing windows and repairing the
roof, cleaning out the basement and preparing supper, scrubbing
the kitchen floor and mowing the lawn, playing table tennis or
rebuking a child's misbehavior—all these actions so common
around the house possess the potential to be sacraments of God's
enduring love to us, revealed through our love for each other.
But if a son can't see the love of God shining through his father's
life at the altar of his father's table or desk or workbench at
home, that son may not choose to find God's love at the altar of
his father's church.

To make our faith in God a constant in our children's experience, they need to see that faith never takes a holiday. Faith never despairs, because the God in whom we believe is faithful. He's the God who *is,* not *was.* His name, given to Moses in the burning bush, is an eternal affirmation of being: "I am who I am" (Exodus 3:14). He's the God whom Abraham knew as *Jehovah-jireh,* the God-who-provides. We know him as the God of Providence; thus, for such a God there's never an emergency. In his divine vocabulary, the word "accident" simply doesn't exist. But it does little good for us to talk like this unless our children see us put to the test and still believing.

As fathers, most of us are concerned that our sons learn the value of thrift, and so we take them to a local bank and open an account in their names. We want them to learn to save money, to earn interest, to make wise investments. I believe that there's a useful analogy here for us to consider. Ever notice how many banks or savings institutions use the terms of faith? Bankers Trust, Provident Savings Bank, Fidelity Mutual Savings and Loan? In the same way that we entrust our financial earnings for safekeeping and investment to these banks, so God expects us to do the same with the good gifts he's given to us. As we demonstrate our commitment to him, God pays interest on faith's investment by adding faith to faith. He never leaves us stranded with devalued currency, and we can never overdraw our account.

But God does allow times of stress in our lives. As our children observe how we behave in these difficult periods, they'll judge for themselves whether or not believing in God makes any difference to us. If our children see us strong in faith, they'll be encouraged to believe for themselves; but if they see us withdrawing all our deposits and abandoning the vault of God's riches—as if in a panic—then they'll decide that God's promises aren't worth the paper they're written on!

You've probably had lots of opportunities to demonstrate your trust in God's faithfulness and his unfailing promises. Certainly I have. Let me share a couple of instances with you. Ordinarily, the Long Island Expressway doesn't seem like an ideal place to commune with God. Stretching from the East River to Peconic Bay, some eighty miles or so, the notorious LIE is sometimes called "the world's longest parking lot." Traffic clogs its six lanes at all hours. One of the jaw-dropping sights for a first-time visitor to New York City is a traffic jam on the Long Island Expressway at one o'clock in the morning. Yes, it's a crowded, dangerous highway, not the best place for sanctified reverie while cruising along on automatic pilot. In fact, whenever I come roaring up the ramp and onto the LIE, I'm usually hunched over the wheel like Richard Petty at Daytona Beach.

On one hot July morning in particular, during the heat of morning rush-hour congestion, I was driving Don to New York City, where he'd catch a Trailways bus to the Adirondack mountains, in upstate New York. We'd left Stony Brook before 7 A.M., plenty of time to get to the Port Authority Terminal by ten. But as the eight o'clock news came on the radio, I suddenly realized that I didn't know exactly where I was. You know the sensation? You've taken the same road a thousand times, but just at that precise instant, you can't identify any landmarks. Furthermore, what's so scary is the knowledge that you've been virtually unconscious for the past few minutes.

No, I didn't know where I was. But with my mind in neutral, I was acutely sensitive to something else. In a way I'd never known before, my mind was totally rid of every distracting thought—the traffic, my son's trip, the work facing me when I returned home; none of these occupied my mind. In this unaccountable openness, I felt words taking shape. I can't say that I *heard* a voice. Rather, I sensed a kind of communication, like the etching of language on sheetmetal. The message was this: "I'm going to teach you something today." That's all. At first, I felt like the man in the after-shave commercial a while back—slapped in the face and replying, "Thanks, I needed that." I shook myself out of my vacant-minded state, but as I did, the words, "Thank you, Lord," formed on my lips. And from somewhere deep within me, this prayer was added: "Whatever you have to teach me, make it possible for Don to learn with me."

In a flash my disorientation disappeared. I knew where we were, just approaching the exits for Manhasset's "Miracle Mile" of fine stores, one of Lory's favorite haunts. Then my eyes focussed, and I saw that the needle on the radiator temperature gauge had rocketed past the boiling point. I knew what was about to happen.

"Please, God, not out here on the Expressway!"

For reasons none of us who use the LIE can comprehend, the busiest highway in America has not one service area. An abandoned car is soon ravaged by roaming bandits who strip it and leave it half-dead. Here we were, trapped in a car with a radiator about to go off like Old Faithful. An opening in the lanes of traffic allowed me to steer off at the exit. As the car changed direction, my son woke from sleep. "What's happening, Dad?"

"God's going to teach us something, Don," I told him. "Let's try to be ready for his lesson."

Now, before you assume anything about my saintliness, you've got to understand my temperament. For a long time, the Lord's been struggling with me to overcome my worst trait, the really ugly side of my character. It's a downright mean and brooding temper. Not the kind that goes off like a bomb and then settles quickly but the hidden kind that stays below the surface of things, then erupts to engulf me and everyone around me. It's like a volcano or an earthquake, and its after-shocks keep on rumbling for days. A random breakdown in my automobile is just the sort of incident I need to set off seismographs at record-breaking readings. What causes my vesuvian rages is the helplessness I feel whenever matters get out of control. I like to be on top of things, to have everything in order. In the routine affairs of life, I can usually keep my equilibrium. But then something goes wrong, like misplacing a set of keys or forgetting to record a check in the balance book. Almost at once, I can begin to feel my world giving way beneath me.

But, as I've already told you, what really reduces me to rubble is any kind of mechanical problem. When something goes wrong with the car or the furnace or the washing machine, my sudden helplessness grinds away at my ego, at my sense of manhood, at my posture as a strong, self-reliant individual. Even though I know it's as phony as a Hollywood shootout, the image of myself takes over. The result, too often, has been that I've made an utter fool of myself.

The only reason it didn't happen that July morning is that I'd been given a gracious word of caution: "I'm going to teach you something today." As the Plymouth station wagon limped and shuddered to a halt on the apron of a Shell station—the only garage along the LIE's service road for miles—I could feel a calm coming over me. Immediately steam burst through the hood, and Don sat waiting for the expected explosion within. But it didn't come.

We waited an eternity for the heat to subside so that we could open the hood and get at the trouble. Meanwhile the commuter traffic kept the only attendant too busy to concern himself with our problem. But at just the same moment that I lifted the hood, a lull in the gasoline line allowed him to come over and examine the car. "Looks like nothin' but a busted belt, mister. But I ain't got time to fix it till this traffic lets up," he told me. That was fine, I replied; I'd leave the car and pick it up later in the morning. Could he direct us to the nearest Long Island Railroad depot?

"Sure, but you'll have to take a taxi to get there."

A call to a local taxi company got us a cab to the Port Washington depot. As we jumped from the taxi, a New York-bound train was just pulling in. We boarded and rode in air-conditioned comfort to Penn Station, a few blocks from the bus terminal. Don made his bus with time to spare. As he boarded, he said to me, "Remember, Dad, 'all things work together for good!'"

Now, as I reversed my course, I was beginning to worry about the cost of car repairs. I hadn't set out from home with much more money than the price of Don's bus ticket. Unexpected train and taxi fares, plus a radiator job, maybe . . . Would I have enough money? I knew I didn't possess a Shell credit card. Back on board the LIRR, I counted my money. Six bucks. I still had another taxi to pay.

"That's eight-fifty," the mechanic told me.

I blanched and gulped. Then I noticed a sign behind him: NO CHECKS CASHED. WE HONOR VISA. So do I! I reached into my wallet for my plastic money and smiled. "This has been quite a day for me," I began.

"Yea? Well, don't tell me your troubles. I got enough of my own." He ran my card through the validating machine and handed me the receipt to sign. Before I could explain why my day had been different from his, he was gone to his next job.

I had no troubles to relate, just a glorious lesson God had prepared me to accept. By gracing me with his warning, the Lord had made it possible for me to control my temper. More than that, he'd allowed me to set a quiet example for my older son. In all our potential for turmoil and recrimination, the stupidities of blaming an automobile or taking out frustration on each other, there hadn't been so much as a ruffled moment. Together, Don and I'd learned that it's possible to survive inconvenience without losing dignity or love. Best of all, Don had noticed my uncharacteristic behavior. His parting words to me at the bus terminal were a cautioning reminder to keep on living in the promise of Romans 8:28. *All things? For good?* Yes, if we accept the premise that God's divine purpose is being worked out in our lives according to his will. It's a lesson I needed just then, a lesson I need every day.

But the same God who makes himself known to us on the Long Island Expressway also watches over our comings and goings wherever they take us. As a family, we've traveled around the world, and so we've become fairly accustomed to the minor crises that afflict all tourists. We've had plane bookings canceled by apparent mistake; we've been robbed in Paris and managed to get out of Ethiopia just as a revolutionary war began. In all our travels, however, God has never failed us; in fact, these crises have only served to demonstrate our continuing reliance upon him, thereby increasing our faith.

But the most dramatic incident—the one that's made the most lasting impression upon every member of our family—occurred in Chittagong, Bangladesh, where my sister Jeannie is a missionary. Upon our arrival in this city of nearly one million people, the police had confiscated our passports to guarantee our good behavior. We were to receive them back on a Saturday afternoon, just before departing the next day. Now, to follow what happened next, you need to understand that bureaucratic inefficiency is a way of life in Bangladesh. Decisions can rarely be made by any individual without consultation, and snarl-ups in the simplest official acts are commonplace. Sounds just like America! In this instance, all that went wrong was that the custodians of our passports had shut their office at the police headquarters and gone home for the day before we'd been able to retrieve our documents. Furthermore, the office was double locked, with two different men each possessing one of the two keys. We learned about this problem at ten o'clock Saturday evening, when we were beginning to pack. Jeannie's superior, a missionary named Gene Gurganus, informed me of the situation and invited me to go along with him in an attempt to find the men with the keys to our passports.

To say that I was dismayed is no overstatement; I was crushed. Not having our passports in hand, we'd never be able to continue on our itinerary; Bangladesh's national airline would have no bookings for a party of five before the following weekend. By that time we were scheduled to be in South India and would have missed the chance to visit Nepal and see Mount Everest—not to mention the Taj Mahal! I called our family together. The boys were then 16 and 14, Ellyn 13, all old enough to know the seriousness of our predicament and what it meant to our plans. "We're going to have to pray this one through," I told them, but without conviction. The look on my children's faces tore at my heart, for I could see my own lack of faith reflected in their gaze.

As I joined Gene Gurganus in his Volkswagen van, I said to him, "There's really only one objective here. I'd like to get those passports, but more important, I'd like God to show his power, especially to my kids tonight." We prayed together. Only once in my life have I dared to challenge God to reveal his sovereignty in a specific, unmistakable way. I've always felt—I still feel—that it's presumptuous of puny little me to tell God anything, to demand that he do thus-and-so. But that night in Chittagong, I did it.

Back and forth we went, from the police station to one or another of Chittagong's mazelike settlements. For more than five hours we palavered and negotiated, pleaded and cajoled, argued and harangued with one official after another—including a very nervous teenage Bengali soldier, whose trigger finger never left his automatic weapon. We wandered down alleys between bamboo hovels, among marauding rats, looking for the home of first one man, then the other. In a series of truly miraculous developments, Bengali men with nothing to gain for themselves, took an interest in my plight and spent that night helping me. Well after three o'clock, the two holders of the prized keys opened their respective locks, and from a file cabinet our five green passports fell onto the floor.

I've never felt such surging joy! The Bengalis shared in handshakes and embraces, although none of them would accept any of the money I offered. Only Gene Gurganus understood the deepest reason for my ecstasy. Back at our quarters, Lory turned on the bedside lamp as I entered the room. Without a word I showed her the passports. "Thank God! We've prayed so hard," she said. Then we cried together in tears of relief and praise. I took the children's passports and laid them on their pillows, next to their heads. At dawn, a few hours later, their shouts of delight were all the alarm clock I needed.

This experience is never far from the center of my mind. An old Gospel song speaks of "Precious memories, unseen angels,/ Sent from somewhere to my soul." I treasure these unforgettable memories as valuable checkpoints in my own pilgrimage, as re-

minders to each member of our family that God's grace is unfailing. But we can't prosper spiritually by living in the past, and
nobody's children can thrive on the sentimentality of "Precious
Memories." A father can't nourish his sons on a diet of pre-
digested blessings, passed along at second hand. Life contains
too many bitter moments, too many wrenching disappointments,
for any of us to survive on the strength of somebody else's faith.
The liability of faith-by-proxy becomes particularly apparent in
the face of death.

In his essay "On the Feeling of Immortality in Youth," William Hazlitt wrote, "No young man believes he shall ever die."
Yet the burial service in *The Book of Common Prayer* reminds
us all that "in the midst of life we are in death." So we fathers
must teach our children the facts of life, which include the fact
of death. In this as in everything we teach, we begin by example,
while our sons and daughters are very young. A father walking
with his little boy saw that his son was fascinated by an army of
ants filing along a crack in the sidewalk toward their anthill.
Suddenly the child began stomping on the insects. Quickly his
father rebuked him and told him to leave the ants alone. "But I
saw you killing ants yesterday with a spray gun in the kitchen,
and you told me they were dirty." The father then took time to
explain to his son that every creature has a right to its own
home. "We'd be a nuisance in the anthill because we're too big
for its tiny rooms," he said. "Ants are a nuisance in our homes
because they get into our food; so we have to scare them away
by killing some of them if they invade our house. But as long as
they stay where they belong, there's no reason to kill them."

One of the best means of teaching a child the sanctity of life
and his responsibility for the well-being of others is by giving
him a pet to care for. A dog raised from a puppy can grow up
with your son and be both a playful companion and a source of
excellent instruction. The boy learns that his dog has certain
needs not entirely foreign to his own—food, shelter, exercise,
cleanliness, medical care, affection. The boy comes to realize that
having a pet means taking on the obligation to provide these ne-

cessities. He can't go off for the day or for a month of summer camp and not bother to ask, "Who's going to feed my dog?" He learns to sympathize with the hurts and pain of other creatures. Perhaps he also learns something about death.

We've had three dogs in our family. Don claimed the first, a short-haired mutt who wandered into our back yard and stayed. Don was about eight years old and very eager to take on the responsibility for the dog he named Duchess. He did well by her; but unfortunately, she became ill and died at a veterinarian's clinic. Her death was the first chill to touch our family. I can't say that we mourned for Duchess; we hadn't kept her very long. But Don and I had a serious talk about death, our first such conversation, and what it means to people and to dogs. I don't think that we did any injustice to Christian theology by comforting each other with the thought that, if God made dogs for his pleasure—as Genesis 1 and Psalm 148 tell us—and if heaven is the place where God wants all his creatures to be with him, happy and praising him, then probably Duchess belongs there too.

We had to make the humane decisions to destroy our next two dogs, and so their deaths came as no surprise. One was a purebred Yorkshire terrier named Hylton Treasure but nicknamed Thrumpley by his previous owners, Tom and Lovelace Howard. Thrumpley was a dear little animal until he became aged and senile, losing his powers of self-control, unable even to keep his hind toenails from catching in his long coat. In his helplessness, he became too vicious for any of us to handle him, even to free him from himself. Our decision to put him out of his own misery—opening to him the gates of larger life, as I told Tom—provoked several family conversations about death and euthanasia, the whole controversy over mercy-killing.

But our third dog's death was by far the hardest. We'd taken Gretel as a puppy, tiny enough to hold in the palm of one hand, and raised her to the age of thirteen. Her mixed breeding, collie and German shepherd, gave her a perfect temperament with children. She was the extra teammate in our family soccer games, a favorite companion on an afternoon run. As she grew older and lame, she contented herself with cheering from the sidelines, so that her barking became a cause for confinement during Stony Brook's home games. At last she was struck by a car and broke a leg. The veterinarian's report was bad news: "There's no way an old dog like this can survive an operation. It's best to put her away." We were heartsick at losing a good friend; but again, we used Gretel's life and death and the happiness she'd brought us as a means of weighing the importance of all God's creatures, especially those of us made in God's own image.

This leap from the death of a pet to the death of a human being shouldn't be either incongruous or insulting, especially as perceived by a child. Some young children, of course, experience the death of their parents or other family members, schoolmates or neighbors, and must face it early in life. Most children, however, never know death except in their pets, until the day a grandparent or elderly acquaintance dies. As their father, I'm glad my children had known something of death's inescapable reality through their pets before the sudden death of their grandfather, my dad.

He died in his sleep on a Friday night in November 1973, stricken by a cerebral hemorrhage just before his sixtieth birthday. As we arrived at the church where his funeral service would be conducted, I took first Don and Kevin, then later Ellyn, to stand by his open casket. Together we shed our private tears, each for his own reasons. Then we went to a room elsewhere in the church and talked about the meaning of death to a believer in Jesus Christ. Only a week before Dad's death, I'd stood in the bass section of a community chorus and sung Brahms's "German Requiem." This masterwork had been written on the occasion of the composer's mother's death—an interesting item in the program notes, but not particular to me; both my parents were in seeming good health. I couldn't have known at the time that God was using the experience of singing Brahms's "Requiem" to prepare me for my own sorrow. Its text sings out Brahms's belief in

the Christian hope, the triumph of life over death. The text also
makes clear something I'd never before realized, that for most of
us, death is our only portal to eternal life. Enoch and Elijah may
have been transported into the presence of God in very special
ways; unless we live to see the Second Coming of our Lord Jesus
Christ, however, our entry into eternity must be through the
grave.

But the words that gripped me as I sang Johannes Brahms's
music weren't the familiar verses of 1 Corinthians, "Death, O
where is thy sting? Grave, where is thy triumph?" Instead I
heard, as for the first time, a passage from James 5:7–8 as ren-
dered in the text used by Brahms:

Now, therefore, be patient, O my brethren,
Unto the coming of the Lord.
See how the husbandman waits for the precious fruit of the
      earth,
And hath long patience for it,
Until he receive the early rain and the latter rain.
So be ye patient.

Meditating on this theme of planting and harvest, I began to understand what Jesus was teaching his disciples when he said that
"unless a kernel of wheat falls to the ground and dies, it remains
only a single seed. But if it dies, it produces many seeds" (John
12:24). This is the ultimate truth about abundant life, possible
only through the paradox of losing-in-order-to-find. The very
next weekend, my father's temporal life had ended so that his
eternal life could begin. His body had to be planted like a seed
in order that he might be harvested by the Lord of the Harvest
himself.

While I couldn't express all this to my children at that time, I
hoped that they'd understand what needed to be said in public
to those who came for comfort to my father's funeral. I wanted
both my children and my father's friends to realize that this moment of death is the critical test of faith for any Christian. My
father had often remarked that, in his role as officiating minister

at scores of funerals, he'd seldom met undertakers who were
believers. "I guess they've seen too many Christians just as shattered by death as unbelievers," he'd say. "What good does it do
to talk about 'the blessed hope' if it doesn't work when you need
it?" These, then, were the few words spoken in a spirit of grief
tempered by that hope:

> At a time of personal crisis, we recall many half-forgotten
> memories preserved in the privacy of our hearts and homes.
> But a service such as this isn't private. By its very nature it has
> become a statement of something. By your presence you are
> witnessing to your respect and affection for a man you know
> and love. For this we are very grateful.
> As his family, we also wish to take the occasion of my father's
> funeral to offer our witness.
> My father always reminded Christians at the passing of a fel-
> low believer that we are instructed to sorrow but not as those
> who have no hope.
> Expressions of loss and bereavement are natural at a time like
> this. But we must remember—we must always remember—that
> our tears are for *ourselves!*
> My father did not see the sunrise last Saturday morning. In-
> stead, he saw the Son. He is in his presence eternally. Which
> of us would wish to bring him back?

For faith in Jesus Christ to take on real significance, it must
become the personal possession of every man and boy. Before
their grandfather's funeral, my sons had never looked squarely
into the future and seen themselves dead. Now they'd been con-
fronted by the grave and by the only hope that conquers the fear
of death. They were ready to experience personally what the
Bible calls being "born again"—the springing forth of new life in
Christ through faith. That moment of commitment, when a son
expresses his own faith in God, equals the joy a father feels on
his son's day of birth.

But such a moment can't be compelled. Like natural birth, the
New Birth will come in its own good time; it can't be rushed or

forced by our parental desire. Indeed, our very anxiety over a
son's spiritual indifference or hostility can be the cause of his
stubborn delay in accepting God's salvation through Jesus
Christ. Lory and I know whereof we speak. Of all our children,
Kevin was the slowest to commit himself to Jesus Christ. He'd
gone to Sunday School and Christian Service Brigade, to Vacation Bible School and summer camp, to a Christian school called
Stony Brook. He wasn't a rebel, but it was quite clear that he
wasn't yet a believer either. We were concerned about his leaving home for college without settling the issue of Christ's place
in his life; yet neither Lory nor I knew what more we could do,
without antagonizing him.

Two people entered Kevin's life who tipped the balance away
from indifference. In his senior year at Stony Brook, Kevin accepted the invitation of his classmate Ned Graham to spend a
part of their spring vacation at Ned's home in Montreat, North
Carolina. Ned's father happened to be at home during those
days, and so Kevin became acquainted with Billy Graham as a
host and friend. What first impressed Kevin was the low-keyed,
unsanctimonious nature of the Grahams' family life. A grace before meals, yes, and a brief prayer after Bible reading; but no sermons, no altar calls. On a couple of occasions during those days,
Billy Graham took a walk with Kevin through the mountainside
woods, talking with the boy about his aspirations, sharing with
him the importance of Jesus Christ in his own life. "He's real,"
Kevin announced upon returning home, a tribute to the way in
which a man greatly used by God throughout the world could
nonetheless give himself to a teenage boy still looking for the answer to life's greatest question.

Even so, Kevin had made no public commitment to Christ by
the time he enrolled at the University of North Carolina. But the
first time Lory and I visited him at Chapel Hill that freshman
year, he came rushing out of his dormitory to our car, greeting us
with these words, "It's all real to me now. I really believe." Then
he turned to me and said, "Dad, I know now you can't be a luke-
warm Christian. It's all or nothing."

What had made the difference? The culmination of many
influences, I'm sure. In the setting of that large university, far
from home and its secure Christian environment, so long taken
for granted, Kevin had found that it wasn't enough to depend on
his parents' faith. He needed a real experience with Jesus Christ
that he could call his own. He was helped immeasurably by a
man named Mike "Moose" Morris, at that time Area Director for
the Fellowship of Christian Athletes in North Carolina. This
giant of a man, tough and tender at once, spoke to Kevin by his
life. Moose and his wife Cyndy opened their lives to Kevin in a
special way so that he saw in them the kind of vital Christian
faith that couldn't be discounted. What he saw, Kevin at last
reached out for and claimed for himself.

When a son accepts for himself the faith of his father, that decision will have an effect on his behavior and attitudes. It's a personal experience, valid and meaningful to him expressly because
it's his own decision, affecting his own life. What may have once
been only his father's rules, legislated with the powerful authority of God's Word for support, gradually comes to be the son's
own standards. He takes from the example of his father, yes; but
beyond that example, he now takes from the source of his father's
faith, the Word of God itself. He begins to see that what his father has been teaching him, for instance, about honor, integrity,
sexual purity, and self-control isn't just an old-fashioned Puritan
ethic; it's the teaching of Jesus himself.

Once he's confessed his own faith in Jesus Christ, a young man
can begin to listen and really hear the lies being spoken in the
name of human freedom and self-gratification: "If it feels good,
do it." He can begin to assess for himself the bankruptcy of
secularism's equivocating ethics: "Just so long as it doesn't hurt
anybody else." He can see through the pretense and false sophistication that demands a trial period of living together before
marriage. He can recognize that all the smart talk about marriage's being an outdated convention of the middle class is just a
nervous cover-up for an unwillingness to commit oneself wholly
to somebody else "till death us do part." He can enter freely into

a loving relationship with a young woman without needing to use her as a sexual guinea pig for his experimentation. If their love leads to marriage, he can rejoice in knowing God's pleasure in marriage and the growth of families; therefore, marriage is sacred and sexual intercourse a sanctifying act between husband and wife. Its physical union speaks of an unbreakable spiritual union between those whom God has joined together; "signifying unto us," as the wedding ceremony states, "the mystical union that is between Christ and his Church." Hugh Hefner and Larry Flynt and Helen Gurley Brown and other advocates of sexual license may not understand this mystery, but that's their loss. We have no reason to scrounge off the menu of scavengers when we've been invited to feast at the King's own banquet.

Of course, the time to talk to your sons about sexuality, physical desires, and God's blessings upon marriage comes long before courtship. Under the widespread influence of television, motion pictures, and popular songs, a child of ten may be singing in French, *"Voulez-vous coucher avec moi ce soir?"* and have no idea of the English translation. On the other hand, no realistic parent today can afford to assume the innocence or lack of curiosity of any ten-year-old regarding sex. Naïveté and ignorance, yes; to an astonishing degree, even among those teenagers whom pollsters delight in calling "sexually active," gross ignorance of anatomy and its natural bodily functions prevails. This is why so many teenage girls become pregnant, much to the surprise of their boyfriends and themselves. With initial moral or religious scruples cast aside, youthful ignorance of the human body becomes their next worst enemy.

With so much visual and aural imagery of licentious sex all around us—on TV, on lavatory walls, in magazines, in songs— Christian parents in particular need to deal directly with the anatomy and its functions. We can't afford to be coy or cute; we can't avoid the issue or be embarrassed by it; most especially, we can't pass it off as somebody else's job to inform our children.

So Christian parents need to be alert to the need to instruct their children about sexuality, sexual behavior, and sexual morality, all in the light of their Christian convictions. This need manifests itself at ever earlier ages and under increasingly alien influences. The day on which I wrote these lines, my wife came home from her elementary school with the news that some of her first-grade pupils are using the expression "making it," while some of their classmates complain that those boys and girls are "talking sexy." *In first grade!* Their curiosity is natural and must be treated so; but it must also be channeled into constructive attitudes toward sexual responsibility.

I remember my own fragmentary sex education. It wasn't a topic for casual discussion in my home, but one evening when I was about ten years old, my father and I went to a revival meeting being held in a tent. It was an old-fashioned, sawdust-trail camp meeting with a country preacher who did a lot of hollering and sweating. I don't remember anything else about the meeting, except that some time during this sermon, the preacher told a story about "an unwed mother." It was a phrase I'd never heard before, although in my mind it somehow seemed to connect with the Virgin Birth—another phrase I didn't understand, in spite of all the times I'd heard it used in church. On the way home I asked my father what the words "unwed mother" meant. He told me in a rather sketchy way, but I could sense that he was rather uncomfortable about my question. I never asked him or anyone else again. In grade ten, my Canadian high school curriculum included those separate classes in health education I've already mentioned; that was the extent of my formal instruction. The rest I learned by threats and warnings from the pulpit or by furtive experimentation. It's not a method to be recommended.

Far better for Christian fathers to instill in their sons a realization that sexual responsibility begins with respect for one's own body—to which the corollary must be respect for the dignity of other human beings also. When Christians finally accept as God's truth what Peter Gillquist calls "the physical side of being spiritual," we'll understand better St. Paul's words,

Do you not know that your body is a temple of the Holy Spirit, who is in you, whom you have received from God?

You are not your own; you were bought at a price. Therefore honor God with your body (1 Corinthians 6:19–20).

Here's the point: These bodies which God has given us are important to him, not merely as flesh-and-blood containers for
something mysterious called the "soul," but for their own sakes.
We've been given something so precious that, when God chose
to reveal himself to his Creation, he did so in the form and shape
of a human body—embryo, fetus, infant, toddler, teenager, man!
In that body he lived and loved and died; in that body,
gloriously resurrected, he was exalted to the presence of the Father. Our bodies are the closest tangible connection we have
with divinity because the Person of Jesus of Nazareth is the only
concrete form in which anyone has ever seen God face to face.
Knowing this, can we treat our bodies—or anyone else's—
cheaply? Can we sell out our personal dignity or desecrate the
temple of God for a thrill? Or can we instead learn to use our
bodies as they were intended? Can we preserve the gestures and
acts of love, expressed sexually in marriage, as the signs and
symbols of divine love?

Fathers to sons, mothers to daughters, but also in openness as
a family, the wonderful and holy reality of sex can be
discussed. Our teaching must be positive and well-balanced, taking account of the body's potential both for creating joy and for
causing wretchedness. For their part, our children should have
no doubt as to their obligations to God, to us as their parents,
to those for whom they care, and to themselves. A son needs to
know, objectively and without threat, what consequences he will
face if he cheapens God's gift of sexuality; a daughter should be
taught the same lesson. In matters as serious as these, it pays to
be candid and utterly blunt, so that there's no cause for misunderstanding. If a son disregards your teaching of Christian moral
principles regarding sex and chooses to live by the permissive
and promiscuous sexual mores of our time—for instance, living
with a woman without bothering about the vows of marriage—he
must be told the consequences of his decision: You will continue
to welcome your son to your home; his friends will come under

the common benediction of your love for him. But he must know that he and his partner may not live under your roof as though it were a whorehouse; you and his mother will not serve as pimp and madam to his fornication. The words may cut deeply, and so they should, because they are the precise terms to describe what God has judged as immoral. Your son may not like the language, but he would never respect you for approving of his sin.

Still another reason for inculcating a Christian standard for sexual behavior is to maintain the highest possibilities for a successful marriage as the foundation of a Christian home. A son must be warned that indiscriminate sexual activity before marriage creates an addiction to erotic memories almost impossible to overthrow. Because sexual relations produce an intimacy that's more than physical, sexual experience enters the realm of deepest psychological reality; there it clings to the memory forever. The mind retains every recollection of love, every searing moment of lust and its fulfillment. Today's amoral sophisticates may think it's chic for one lover to say to the other, in the act of intercourse, "You tell me who you're thinking about, and I'll tell you . . ." But that's no way to begin a marriage. A young man and his bride deserve more than the tragedy expressed in an old Korean aphorism, "Same pillow, different dreams." That's why it's so essential that your son choose a young woman to be his wife who will share his faith and hope as well as his love. For it takes all three—faith, hope, and love—to make a secure Christian marriage.

All too soon the time comes when your son will want to talk with you about his romance with a special girl and his intentions to marry her. At first, it may seem so incongruous—this gangling oaf who can scarcely remember to brush his teeth in the morning —speaking about marriage! Then you may recall that you were already married at his age, and perhaps only half as wise as he! If your relationship with your son is sound, you probably already know the young woman on whom he's set his heart. No doubt, you gladly approve of his choice because, for reasons not so mysterious for us to comprehend, she resembles in some ways his own mother, your wife. If your son has lived in a balanced Christian home, he's seen in your marriage the tenderness of abiding affection and respect, as well as the wholesome and glad-hearted warmth of love that touches and treasures each other. Obviously, he wants the same for himself.

Not long ago, it seems, I drove my son Don on his first date, to a seventh-grade square dance. Ten years later, in the spring of 1979, as he and I were taking a run through the woods in beautiful Chapel Hill, he told me that he knew he wanted to marry Belinda Polk. His announcement came as no shock. On the day we'd arrived to bring him home at the end of his freshman year, he'd told us, "Mom and Dad, I met the best-looking girl at UNC last night!" Throughout the following year, their paths never seemed to cross; but at the beginning of their junior year at Carolina, they began dating regularly. As seniors, they were considered a steady couple.

"That's great, Don," I panted as I plodded along. "You know Mom and I love Belinda very much. But let's slow down so I can ask you a couple of questions."

We walked along together, father and son. "Do you love Belinda enough to commit yourself to her for the rest of your life?"

"I sure do, Dad."

"Does she love you the same way?"

"She tells me she does, and I believe her."

"Then, Don, I've got just two more questions to ask. Of all the interests you have in common, where does Jesus Christ fit in?" He told me of their times of prayer together and their sharing with other Christian students in worship and fellowship.

"One last word: Are you willing to be like Christ to Belinda, to give your life for her, if necessary?"

"You know I am," Don told me. On July 5, 1980, Belinda and he were married.

Throughout this book, I've been assuming that your son has come to share your faith in Jesus Christ, establishing his own personal relationship with God. So it must be for every man—

every father and son. No matter how much we care about the other, none of us can make another man's decisions for him; none of us can drag another man and make him kneel in obedience before God. In Ezekiel 18, the prophet conveys God's concern that fathers and sons should understand each other's personal responsibility: "For every living soul belongs to me," says God, "the father as well as the son—both alike belong to me. The soul who sins is the one who will die" (Ezekiel 18:4). The righteous father whose son persists in unrighteousness must recognize that his son's doom rests upon his son's own head; likewise, the righteous son of an unrighteous father will not be held accountable for his father's sins. Every man must account for his own relationship with God; it's not a reckoning on which any of us defaults.

On the surface, perhaps, this may sound a little too pat, a little too simple. We'd like to find an alternative to suggest to God. We'd like to have him reconstruct the universe so that, either we're automatons without any freedom to disobey the power that controls us, or else we're morally weightless creatures, totally free from the constraints of God's law. But that's not how God designed human beings. Because God has made us free to choose our own destiny, there comes a time in every person's experience when that choice must be made, its consequences accepted. As C. S. Lewis writes in *The Great Divorce,*

> There are only two kinds of people in the end: those who say to God, "Thy will be done, and those to whom God says, in the end, *"Thy* will be done." All that are in Hell, choose it.

As long as God preserves in us the power of choice, some of us human beings will choose to reject God's way in preference for our own; some of our children are going to rebel against God.

Many godly men have known this anguish. The Old Testament patriarchs themselves had sons whose sin, like Lamech's vengeance, multiplied the sin of Cain. Noah's youngest son Ham made his father a laughingstock and a scandal. Abraham beseeched the Lord, "If only Ishmael might live under your blessing!" (Genesis 17:18); yet Ishmael and his sons continue to live in hostility toward the remaining descendants of Abraham to this day. Isaac's firstborn Esau sold his birthright for a lentil stew; Isaac's younger son Jacob cheated both his father and brother out of the paternal blessing. In his own turn, Jacob suffered the deceit and corruption of wicked sons. His eldest, Reuben, committed incest with his father's concubine, while Judah sold his own brother Joseph into slavery and then lied to their father. In the days of Israel's judges, Eli's sons, Hophni and Phinehas, were notoriously wicked, so much so that the name of Phinehas' son, born at the news of his father's death, has come down to us as a synonym for departed glory: Ichabod. Likewise, Samuel's two sons, Joel and Abiah, ignored their father's example and "did not walk in his ways. They turned aside after dishonest gain and accepted bribes and perverted justice" (1 Samuel 8:3). Saddest of all is the lament of King David after his son Absalom's revolt:

O my son Absalom! My son, my son Absalom! If only I had died instead of you—O Absalom, my son, my son! (2 Samuel 18:33)

How seldom we read of kings and princes like Jehoshaphat, who "walked in the ways of his father Asa and did not stray from them; he did what was right in the eyes of the Lord" (1 Kings 22:43).

No Christian family can afford to pride itself on being immune to the tragedy of a child's disbelief. Preachers, evangelists, missionaries, outstanding Christian laypersons—men and women of unswerving commitment to Jesus Christ—are all too frequently burdened by knowing that their own sons and daughters have deliberately turned their backs on Jesus Christ. "Show me your God," says the son of missionary parents, "and I'll spit in his eye!" The daughter of a Christian statesman cries out in rage against her father, "I know how I'll get even—I'll get pregnant! That'll drive my father wild!"

Adolescent rebellion against the faith of our fathers is a common theme in fiction and drama, a common subject of public dismay in our pulpits and editorials. This same spirit of rebellion underscores the most poignantly human story Jesus ever told, the

parable of the Prodigal Son. But even its retelling may seem
remote, unlikely to be real—until one knows in his gut this
cruelest of all pains, until a son's rejection of God and his love
strikes at the very heart of a Christian home. What are we to
do, then, if a son upon whom we've lavished a father's devotion
takes that legacy of love and throws it in our face? What happens when he debases the teaching he's received and rejects the
prayers he once recited as a child? What are we to do when the
best we've done seems to have turned to ashes?

A few years ago, I'd just finished preaching a Sunday morning
sermon on Jesus' parables in Luke 15. I'd stressed the father's
unquenchable love and his willingness to disgrace himself publicly by running to greet his offending son. At the churchdoor I
was met by a father wracked with grief and anger. "You don't
know anything about it," he exclaimed, "nobody in this church
knows!" He left the church in tears, dismissing any attempt to
console him. Two days later, I received this letter in the mail:

Dear Mr. Lockerbie,
How wonderful that your sons believe! But our son doesn't believe in any god except those demons that come in the shapes
of pills and syringes. So what can you possibly say to us?
For far too long a time, my wife and I have had to sit and listen to sermons like yours, preached without any basis in experience, without any personal understanding of what it means
to be the parents of a prodigal son. Don't you see, until you've
stood in my shoes, you have no business talking about "a father's unquenchable love"? I'm here to tell you—and every
other idealist—that there comes a time when love has reached
its limits—as it has with me. I won't stand for having you or
anyone else condemn me for saying, "I hate my son and what
he's done to ruin our lives!" Don't think those words come easily, without pain. Don't think I'm insensitive to what those
words mean. For years, I've struggled against saying them. For
years, my wife and I have castigated ourselves, torn our souls
to shreds in self-condemnation. When the first signs of his rebellion against God, the church, our family's standards of

honor, or even simple common decency began to show themselves, we spent hours and hours examining ourselves to see
what might be wrong with the way we were bringing up our
son. Later, we spent thousands of dollars for therapy and de-
toxification in an attempt to restore his mind and body.

Perhaps—we thought—we were being too hard on him, expecting him to attend Sunday School and church with us, requiring him to memorize Scripture as part of our family devotions,
insisting that he respect our reverence for God and his Word.
So, for a time, we made attending church optional—and he
repaid us by smashing the church windows and spraying ob-
scene graffiti on the walls. We eliminated our mandatory
Scripture memorization—and he gave us instead the depraved
lyrics of lewd popular songs to fill our ears. We stopped demanding that he respect at least his parents' rights to worship
—and he rewarded our recognition of his rights by mockery
and profanity.

But when we realized that our attempts at meeting him half-
way had failed, and when we tried to regain our authority
over him, he laughed at us for being fools enough to think that
he'd ever come back under our control.

Then this stricken father concludes his letter with these de-
spairing words:

So we've decided to waste no more time and no more money
on trying to prevent his self-destruction. If that's his preference, so be it. We take as God's damnation upon our son the
warning of Solomon: "He that being often reproved hard-
eneth his neck shall suddenly be destroyed, and that without
remedy."

How would you have done any better?

I've no wish to judge another man in his anguish, yet I wonder
if there isn't something missing from this altogether shattering
account of personal and family torture. Where is the father's admission of his own imperfections? Where's his recognition of
ways in which he and his wife may have contributed to their

son's dereliction? Can it be that this home never knew a petty
quarrel between parents, an act of injustice, or an unreconciled
wrong? Can it be that the acts of goodness were always and only
on the part of the parents and never the son? Or is there present
in this letter an insidious self-righteousness, a pious refusal to
take any share of the blame? What can we learn from this father's pain?

First, we can look at our own behavior to discover what it is
about our relationship with God and our service to Jesus Christ
that so completely alienates that son. For example, it may be
that our spiritual priorities are out of alignment. "My father
should've been a monk," says an unbelieving college student. "If
he wanted to serve God all the time, why'd he bother getting
married and having five kids? He's got no time for us, no time
for Mom, no time for anything but his damned church!" This
son's complaint can be heard over and over among children an-
tagonistic to the faith. Somehow Christian husbands and fathers
have got to learn that God is best served through our wives and
children; and if not through them, then not at all—or, at least, far
less than we suppose, whatever else our achievements may be.
To Christian fathers whose children have been neglected so that
somebody else's soul might be saved, our Lord's stinging words
of rebuke apply: "I was hungry and you gave me nothing to eat,
I was thirsty and you gave me nothing to drink" (Matthew
25:46). In too many instances, our own sons are taken for
granted and become those whom Jesus calls "the least of these
brothers of mine." No wonder that they scorn a faith whose practice has left them outside its most fundamental principle, a father's love for his child.

Or perhaps our expectations have been too high, our punishment too harsh. Another son, long since decided against his father's faith, explains his reason. "When I was twelve, my father
caught me smoking out behind the house. He took me inside and
beat me with his belt, so hard and so long that both of us were
exhausted. He kept saying to me, 'Promise me you'll never smoke
again,' and I kept saying, 'Every time you hit me, I swear I'll
never stop smoking!' My father lost me that day." Here's a com-

mon case of paternal rage and stupid pride being mistaken for
righteous indignation and Christian nurture. What does St. Paul
warn? "Fathers, do not embitter your children, or they will become discouraged" (Colossians 3:21).

Loving discipline never calls for brutality; but a corollary to
that rule is this: Loving discipline is never weak. In the name of
love, some fathers choose not to punish their children physically
for fear of losing a child's love; instead, they rely solely upon
verbal correction and reasoning. "I was whipped so often and so
hard as a boy," a father tells me, "I vowed never to spank my
own children." As a result, his son and daughter are the terror of
any public group upon which their presence is inflicted. They're
unruly, bullying to other children, disrespectful to their parents.
Apparently this father fails to realize that his young children
can't possibly comprehend all the philosophical reasons for obeying him. Their intellectual capacities haven't been sufficiently developed to think through the processes of cause and effect. Children simply can't remember the logical reasons for obedience.
But their physical senses often remember what their minds may
forget, and the recollection of brief but intense pain—a few smart
slaps on the bottom—can produce what logical discourse fails to
engender.

No doubt this was King David's problem. He may have been a
great poet and a mighty warrior, but his sons' record of
lawlessness suggests that David was no model as a father. His
sons were worse than spoiled brats; they were murderous toward
each other and their father. Absalom's insurrection drove his father from the throne. Solomon, who succeeded David lawfully,
executed his brother Adonijah; and for all his vaunted wisdom
and splendor, Solomon foolishly allowed his many pagan wives
to turn him to idolatry. Why did David fail as a father? The
Scriptures give us a hint in a parenthetical comment regarding
Adonijah's upbringing:

(His father had never interfered with him by asking, "Why do
you behave as you do?" He was also very handsome and was
born next after Absalom) (1 Kings 1:6).

In spite of one son's incorrigibility, David seems not to have learned that children need a chastening hand. Ironically, the man who knew how to tend sheep with a rod and staff let his own sons run wild. By neglecting corporal punishment, a father disregards the fact that his children require physical correction as much as they need other physical demonstrations of affection. The father who chooses not to spank his son forfeits the right to hug him also. Both are the prerogatives of love, and you can't have one without the other.

"Love is patient, love is kind . . . it keeps no record of wrongs. . . . It always protects, always trusts, always hopes, always perseveres (1 Corinthians 13:4–7). Could any words more fully represent the enduring quality of fatherlove—the patience by which he strains to hope against hope—than these familiar phrases of St. Paul? "Love never fails," the Apostle goes on. But he would certainly agree that love must sometimes seem cruel in order to be kind. For until a prodigal son can say, "Father, I have sinned," love's most common manifestation—an unconditional welcome home—must be suspended. In Robert Frost's poem, *The Death of the Hired Man*, one person defines *home* as

> the place where, when you have to go there,
> They have to take you in.

But that's a shallow understanding of home. The essence of home can't be reduced to obligation and rights taken for granted. There must also be a willing acceptance of mutual responsibility. When either a father or his son abandons his responsibility to the other, their home as such no longer stands. It can only be rebuilt when repentance leads to forgiveness and restoration. For this to happen, both father and son must come to their senses and recognize that a father is always a father, a son is never less than a son, and what has been lost may yet be found.

Careful self-examination requires us to act upon our spiritual diagnosis, to take the remedy that the Scriptures prescribe, no matter how bitter it tastes. If our failing has been an uncontrollable temper or a foolish preoccupation with business or a callous aloofness to our family's needs, we must confess our sin to God and to those whom we've offended—even to the son who professes not to care. We must then set about rectifying our attitudes and behavior, putting ourselves under the mercy of Christ and his grace. Then we must wait for God to do his part in purging our character of those very traits that alienate us from our loved ones. It won't be easy, it may not happen overnight, but God has promised to renew our minds and spirits. When this is done, no matter how rebellious a son seems, he will not forever scorn what he sees to be true.

This is the hope that the father of every prodigal son must cherish and never give up. As we pray for the power of God to renew our lives, so that same Holy Spirit works upon the conscious and unconscious desires, even of someone who has wandered into hostile territory. In his spiritual desolation, he may be brought face to face with the meaning of Jesus' remarkable teaching about losing-in-order-to-find. Our Lord's conundrum illustrates the nature of paradox, which G. K. Chesterton defined as "truth standing on its head to get attention." The point Jesus makes is simply this: Sometimes losing is the only way to find.

Think of the younger son in the parable. While in his father's house, he had a surfeit of food and all the comforts of home. It was easy to turn his back upon what had always been so readily at hand. For a while he survived on his own resources and the gaiety of his companions; but in time, he squandered all he had. Now sitting in the pig-sty, his stomach gnawing with hunger, he learns that he would gladly settle for a sip from the swill pail and a morsel of pig fodder. Only when his situation has become so desperate does he come to his senses and realize the extent of his losses. The most lowly servant in his father's house has food to spare! Why should he starve to death? When such a son has been brought to the absolute nadir of life—"so far down, he has to reach up to touch bottom," my father used to say—when he knows that he's lost everything he ever had, God the Father

stands waiting, ready to respond to his first indication of repentance, eager to run to the returning son and throw his arms of
love around him, welcoming him home. We too must welcome
home the wastrel and the vagabond, the vagrant and the ne'er-
do-well, the lost sheep and the prodigal.

The road back home is prayer. Sometimes it may seem tedious
and unending, but the New Testament assures us that "the
prayer of a righteous man is powerful and effective" (James
5:16). As Christian fathers, we pray both for the rebel and for
those sons who remain faithful; we pray for our sons as well as
for ourselves. One of my favorite prayers is the famous prayer of
St. Richard of Chichester, first prayed seven hundred years ago,
made popular in its adaptation to the song "Day by Day" from
Godspell:

> Thanks to Thee, my Lord Jesus Christ,
>> for all the benefits which Thou hast given me,
>> for all the pains and insults which Thou hast
>>> borne for me.
> O most merciful Redeemer, Friend, and Brother,
>> may I know Thee more clearly,
>> love Thee more dearly,
>> and follow Thee more nearly.

In uttering this prayer day after day, I'm asking God to help me
become a worthy example for my sons to emulate, a father
whose name my sons are proud to share.

When I was just eleven years old, our family drove from
Toronto to Eastern Ontario, to the region north of the St.
Lawrence River, where my father had been born. We reached
the little villages of Ventnor and Spencerville just before midnight; the residents had long since gone to bed. But Dad needed
directions to find the old homestead, where we were to spend
the night. Reluctantly he stopped at a darkened house and
knocked on the door. After several minutes of waiting, the yard
light came on, and an older man opened his door. I could hear
my father apologizing for the inconvenience; then he identified

himself as the son of Pearson Lockerbie—my grandfather dead for more than a score of years.

"Come in, come in," said the man. "No trouble at all. We knew your father."

That's the greatest legacy a man can leave his son.

D. Bruce Lockerbie is Dean of Faculty at The Stony Brook School, where he has been since 1957. He and his wife Lory are the parents of three grown children, two sons and a daughter. A teacher and educational consultant as well as writer—*Fatherlove* is his thirtieth book—he is also a frequent lecturer at colleges, universities, and seminaries throughout the country.